The Hidden Treasures in Gray Hair

- Adults' Golden Words of Wisdom

Dele Ajaja

> **NOTE**
>
> You or any member of your family who happens to visit the West coast has a room in my house any Day.
>
> Dele ajaja

...late ma-
...and im-

- The teachers who taught me how to read, write, and understand the hidden things.
- And the other elders who counseled me on how to navigate the tricky "waterways" of life.

Cover graphic by Dele Ajaja

Copyright © 2010 Dele Ajaja
All rights reserved.

ISBN: 1-4515-6453-8
ISBN-13: 9781451564532

September 8, 2021

Dear Johannes,

    Thank you again for the good deeds you do. You are truly an outstanding American. The assistance you rendered to me in London in May 2021 rekindled my faith in mankind.

    You are a brother for life.

Compliment of the author.

Dele Ajaja

—CONTENTS—

Opening
Choices and Consequences
   Citations for Youth   vii

Chapter 1:   SUCCESS
            —The Parable of the Yam   1

Chapter 2:   WISDOM
            —The Gift of a Lifetime   19

Chapter 3:   CHARACTER
            —The Authentic Beauty   39

Chapter 4:   ASSOCIATION
            —The Defining Choice   59

Chapter 5:   TIME
            —The Consumable Entity   77

Chapter 6:   ANGER
            —The Sightless Zone   97

Chapter 7:   PRIDE
            —The Pretty and the Monster   115

Chapter 8:   RESPECT
            —The Rebounding Reward   135

Chapter 9:   TOLERANCE
            —The Exploit of the Broadminded 151

Chapter 10: DISCIPLINE
            —The Exceptional Endowment   171

Chapter 11: ACCOUNTABILITY
            —The Inevitable Remuneration 189

Chapter 12:	PERSEVERANCE	
	—The Resolve to Win	209
Chapter 13:	COURAGE	
	—The Attribute of the Valiant	231
Chapter 14:	CITIZENSHIP	
	—The Bequest of the Patriot	249
Chapter 15:	LEADERSHIP	
	—The Humbling Mission	267

Opening

Do you know some adults who cannot use cell phones to send text messages? Such adults probably understand life more than sending messages with those gadgets. Many youths assume they understand life more than adults, because they are more technologically savvy than the adults. They presume they don't need adults' advice when it comes to making choices and decisions. Interestingly, the opposite is the case. Youths need responsible adults' counsel and guidance more than they realize.

Traveling on the road of life becomes tricky sometimes, and it requires experience to endure it. Adults have a wealth of knowledge that youths can learn from. Obviously, young people are smart and understand what they see and do often. However, what about the hidden experiences they need in order to succeed in life, but which are not as readily comprehensible as using cell phones to send texts to friends?

The Hidden Treasures in Gray Hair is a recollection of what I've learned from the dependable adults in my life. This **"youth's companion"** will give youths some ideas on how to enhance their lives by listening to the counsels of the responsible adults in their lives. Such adults include steadfast parents, grandparents, teachers, counselors, prudent role models, community leaders, and the other dependable grown-ups. Experience, they say, is the best teacher. Adults have a lot of experiences they could share with youths, because insight comes with maturity. The young people who listen to the counsels of reliable adults could learn something from them.

In this book I engage my personal experiences and the wisdom I learned from the elders of my ancestral *Yoruba* ethnic group in West Africa, where I grew up. The *Yorubas* are known for expressing their views, thoughts, beliefs, understanding, expectations, and experiences through rich parables and narratives. The youths who pay attention to the elders' golden words of wisdom rarely stumble along the road of life.

CHOICES AND CONSEQUENCES: CITATIONS FOR YOUTH

- Choices and consequences are equal and complementary. Life has a way of giving back an equal amount of consequence for the same amount of choice. You get a beautiful consequence for a beautiful choice, and you get an ugly consequence for an ugly choice.
- Your choices reflect your sense of worth. You have a judicious sense of worth if you make judicious choices, and you have ludicrous sense of worth if you make ludicrous choices.
- It seems like yesterday when I was eight, and I would be eighteen before I know it. Then, I would not be judged by what my parents, teachers, and the community did or did not do, but by the choices I made. People would assume that my parents provided the meals, teachers taught me, and the community provided the school, but I failed to take advantage of those opportunities.
- My tomorrow depends on the aggregate of choices I make today. The days

I arrive on time, pay attention to the teacher, and do my part will add up. The days I cut classes, disrespect the teacher, and act disruptively will add up, too.
- The future will judge me on my own pedestal—not on my parents', teachers', or society's platforms. Life will evaluate me based on the choices I have made. The future will see my destiny in my own hands; it won't recall when it was in my parents' hands or when my teachers had it in their hands.
- Success is not copiously initiated by luck, wishes, or day dreaming. Accomplishment is the consequence of steady, fine choices...and bits of luck, wishes, and day dreaming.
- What I commit or omit today could affect my tomorrow. I will level the hill of responsibility that stands before me today, as tomorrow may come with its own hill. In this way, my life won't be dwarfed by insurmountable hills of responsibilities.
- Nature's statute of limitation will stop my mother from buying me groceries someday; and my father will not clothe me forever. I must step in to dress and nourish myself someday. The chameleon has delivered its baby; the ability to blend with the environment now depends on the baby chameleon.

- You are right if you think life is unfair. Reality is not fair to the intractable youths who mortgage their own good fortune.
- Conclusively, do not be mad at the messengers who say your consequences are as good as your choices get. Parents, teachers, counselors, community leaders, and other tough-love givers are just the couriers who deliver the messages sent by reality.

Chapter 1
SUCCESS—The Parable of the Yam

Don't start life where you are supposed to end it. Life starts with the struggle to achieve and ends with the savoring of the fruits of one's labor. Those who start life from the pleasurable side often finish at the struggle end.

Growing up was tough for me. Elementary school was the toughest. I had no shoes but had to trek to and from school on the dusty and patchy roads. The school district had no busses to transport children, and no one had a car yet in my family. I had several reasons to stay away from school, but Grandma insisted that education was the only way forward.

"Don't worry about the hardship, Son. He who would eat the honey situated in the rock doesn't worry about the edge of the axe he uses for breaking the rock." My grandmother encouraged me to keep trying.

It rained a lot during the rainy season, and it was noticeably cold during the *harmattan*, West Africa's equivalent of a snowless winter. Unfortunately, I had no jacket to fence off the cold, till Uncle Folu gave me an old cardigan. The woolen material was too big for me, but I was contented and appreciative while wearing it, because many of my peers had none.

"You are lucky to have a well-off uncle," said one of the kids in my class, referring to my cardigan.

Drenched to our underwear, the other children and I would run playfully along the road whenever it rained on the way to or from school. Mother Nature sometimes let loose dazzling tropical lightening and deafening thunders, but we did not think much of them. We were inexperienced children who believed that lightening killed only bad people.

We anticipated rain anytime during the raining season. We would cover our notebooks with waterproof nylons. Then, we would sprint lightheartedly and sing innocently in the rain:

It is raining
Play indoors
Away from the rain
Avoid getting wet
Keep away from the cold.

To the wet but happy children, that was just another song composed by the "over-protective" adults to stop us from enjoying ourselves. We did

The Hidden Treasures in Gray Hair

not know any child who had died after stomping the numerous puddles along the streets to the local school.

Unintentionally, I hit my toes on rocks along the streets so many times that I cannot recount the number. It hurt badly, especially when the same toe hit a rock before the previous injury had healed. I stepped on sharp objects occasionally, but I thought that was part of growing up. Grandma would wash and press the injured part with a rag soaked in warm water, and apply penicillin ointment.

"Be careful. Watch the roads carefully next time," my grandmother warned.

I ate half-penny *amala* (plantain paste) with vegetable soup before heading to school in the morning. However, I had no money for lunch most of the time. I ate lunch only when Grandma gave me some *gari*, the cassava flour that I usually soaked in a bottle of water. Several children came to school with their own bottles of *gari*, too. I was hungry at school much of the time, and wondered when things would get better, but Grandma assured me that things would change for good in the future if I stayed with my studies.

"You'll have as much food as you want someday, if you keep going to school," began Grandma. "You'll even have something left for those who have nothing to eat," she consoled me many times when I talked about hunger. I was suspicious of Grandma for suggesting that school would end my hunger someday when she had not gone to school herself.

Grandpa soon solved the mystery of how education could stop hunger. One day, I overheard him talking to *Oga Imisi*, one of my uncles, about the place of education in modern time.

"The D.O. was appointed because he had some education. I had been around longer than him and I probably understood life more than he did, but I wasn't selected to run the district," he lamented. I later found out that D.O. meant the *District Officer*, who oversaw government affairs in the area.

As tough as life was as a child, I could not complain. There was no ground for nagging, because most people in the town faced similar issues. I saw the vicious circle as an advantage. It provided me with the opportunity to see poverty at close range. I did not have to go far to understand hardship. Thus, I yearned for success earnestly.

I knew that life was better for some, but they were too few. I could count the "rich people" in the town on the fingers of my hands. Someone could be considered "rich" just because he had a small-scale business or a *korope*, the small wooden-cabin lorry that transported people and goods from one town to another.

A couple of the small business owners bought cocoa beans from local farmers and resold to bigger merchants from the city. Two men had small

The Hidden Treasures in Gray Hair

sawmills where the locals bought woods for roofing, furniture, and other wooden objects. Other business owners had small supply stores where they sold household items.

Each of the two "richest" individuals in the town had a three-story building. The structures were ordinary and lacked special architectural designs, but that did not stop the owners from being the talk of the town. It wasn't unusual to see children standing near the houses and admiring them.

"Hey! I salute prosperity," some of the youths would say in amazement.

I smiled a lot, as I enjoyed the company of the other kids in my position. There were many of us in my neighborhood and at the local school. A bunch of underprivileged but hopeful children, who accepted life the way it presented itself. We tried to make the best out of every little opportunity we had. We competed over who knew more English words.

We read every book we found from cover to cover, since there were not many of them. Neither the school nor the town had a library. We sometimes wrote or added figures in the sand before copying the final answers on papers. We couldn't afford to waste scarce notebooks for the sketchy parts of our homework.

I wished my family had a small-scale business or a *korope*, so I could be like one of the few "rich people's" children. They wore leather *Cortina* shoes to school and came with lunch money, too. They sported the elegant *trelin* trousers and polyester shirts during the New Year celebration, but I had *Ankara*, the inexpensive low-profile fabric. Grandma bought me a pair of shoes sometime, but I could only wear them on Sundays.

There were only a few "rich" people's children, but they had more influence, and were very popular. The majority of them knew what they were doing, but some allowed their families' fames to get into their heads. *Oyinbo*, the local entrepreneur's son, in particular, did not do well at school. *Oyinbo* was the local name for a white person, but a fair-skinned national shared the title, too.

Oyinbo was failing as we moved on. He ditched school a lot and paid no attention when he was present. He even encouraged other students to disrespect the teacher. In due course, he dropped out of school because of poor grades and a lot of misconduct.

To everyone's surprise, *Oyinbo* wanted to be "rich" like his father, but he did not work hard like him. Regrettably, the modest wealth his father left behind was not enough to enrich his many children. *Oyinbo* ended up not measuring up to his father in terms of accomplishment.

Years later, I could understand when an older neighbor told me the story of how young people could become successful in life without allowing

The Hidden Treasures in Gray Hair

anything to get in their way. It remains one of the most memorable stories I heard from adults.

"I owe my success to paying attention to what mattered, and not to the many distractions of life," started the man. He was a bank manager in the city, and everyone knew that people worked hard to become one. The people in the neighborhood respected him a lot.

"I'll call my story *'the parable of the yam,'*" added the man enthusiastically. He went on to tell the story of how yam started out humbly, germinated quietly, and grew dutifully before becoming a well sought-after commodity that many spent reasonable amounts of money to buy for dinner.

"The farmer cuts a tuber of yam into smaller pieces, and plants each piece inside the mold of soil. Every piece is about to begin a life-circle of struggle and survival," explained the neighbor. I could feel his passion for imparting words of wisdom to a youth who was willing to listen.

"The persistent piece survives, but the relenting one gives up the struggle to survive," he added, sneaking a peek at me, to make sure I was paying attention. Sure enough, I was marveling at the different ways the diverse plants grow—some grow from tubers cut into smaller pieces and planted in the soil; some from stems, cut and stuck in the soil; and others grow from the seeds planted in the soil.

"The small piece of yam planted in the soil must work hard before growing and becoming a desirable tuber," I contributed, so my neighbor would not be the only one talking.

"You bet, the piece of yam suffers from a great deal of heat; remember, it is buried in the soil, away from air and sunshine," continued the man. I could tell that he was happy that I was showing interest. I knew that his son did not show interest in his stories.

"Although the little piece of yam takes a lot of heat, it is tenacious. The urge to survive pushes it to continue with the germination process," clarified the older man. The life-circle of a plant was not strange to me. After all, my grandfather was a farmer, and I had gone to his farm many times. However, I had never linked how plants grow with how humans achieved success.

It is amazing how much knowledge one can unveil about something he assumes he knows so much about if he looks at it differently. I started thinking about the possibility that people sometimes did not know enough about something though they assumed they knew it all. Now, I was learning something interesting about the plant that I had seen many times, and had taken for granted all of the time.

"The piece of yam starts to decompose due to intense heat and the microorganisms in the soil. The yam hides in the soil, away from the prying eyes of passersby, struggling to survive, without exposing itself to the world yet," explained the storyteller.

The Hidden Treasures in Gray Hair

This is becoming interesting, I thought, sitting and looking intensely at the man as I placed my chin in my hands. I couldn't have spent my evening in a better way than paying attention to the words of wisdom from a successful adult.

"The piece of yam, thought to be decomposing, is actually getting ready to germinate. Tiny foliage sprouts from it and begins its upward journey toward the surface after some time," said the man, gesturing with his two hands moving from the ground upward.

I could imagine how the man's story related to the youth who set himself aside from the distractions of modern time and tried to succeed, regardless of the hardship he faced. It appeared that I had something in common with the story. That was why I was so excited for him to continue.

It was clear that the man had found a good listener in me as he continued his story gleefully. I tried to imagine how many times he had told the story, and how many youths had learned from it. Something told me that any youth who did not learn from the story would probably learn from nothing.

"Remember that the piece of yam remains inside the soil, away from view, without seeking attention from passersby? It continues with the same trend without asking for unnecessary attention as it sprouts upward," said the bank manager.

"For the first time, passersby would notice the yam as it sprouts to the surface, but they won't think much of it, because it is a humble foliage signaling its intention to grow and become something out of the numerous plants in the bush," maintained the man, who was trying to teach me the lesson of a lifetime.

I realized early in life that youths could learn a lot from adults. Although I sometimes figured out certain things before the adults around me, I did not doubt that I had a lot to learn from them.

"Gradually, the little foliage starts growing taller, and many don't even take it seriously yet. Later, the yam's leafy, flexible, long stem starts clambering and twining around the pole staked by the farmer for that purpose.

"Suddenly, the yam's leaves start covering the whole area around the mold of soil. Then, people start taking it seriously, because they now understand that a big tuber is taking shape inside the mold," added the man.

My face glowed with enthusiasm. *That's what Grandma meant*, I thought proudly inside of me. I recalled that my grandmother admonished my cousins and me to pay attention to education and our efforts would pay off someday. The man was not done with his story yet, but it was already making a lot of sense to me.

"The luxuriantly growing yam impresses the farmer. He takes care of the spaces around it; removes the unwanted weeds and applies manure. It is now clear that the farmer is interested in the useful plant, and not the valueless weed.

The Hidden Treasures in Gray Hair

"Passersby are now paying more attention to the growing yam. Everyone understands that it will fetch the farmer good money at the marketplace someday," he said with a smile across his face. The bank manager knew he was getting my full attention, as I gazed at him wittingly. Clearly, the two of us were having a blast.

"The yam is not even revealing its best part yet. People see the leaves outside, but the edible tuber continues to grow bigger and bigger inside the soil, without showing off. The world is yet to see the best part of the yam," said the banker almost poetically.

"I can relate the story to young people and their parents," I suggested. The man gestured to me to continue the thought. He seemed satisfied with the two of us saying things that reflected that the exchange was mutually beneficial.

"The yam is the child," I began, "and the happy farmer is the parent or guardian. The adult is proud and willing to invest in the child when he does well at school…I mean, when the child pays attention to his teacher, without getting into trouble or calling unnecessary attention to himself."

"You are right," he complimented before continuing with the best part of the story. I could not wait to hear that part, because the component of the story that taught people a lesson usually lurked in the end.

"The yam tuber beneath the surface will become big enough someday, and the farmer will dig it up, wash it, and take it to the marketplace. Then, people will come to the market with money. Guess what? The yam will go to the highest bidder in the end."

"Whoa!" That was all I could say as the storyteller concluded. I knew he was yet to explain his own part of how the story related to people, as storytellers in that region did, but I knew what he had left to say. I waited patiently for him to bring out the wisdom he tried to pass on with the story.

"Many young people allow modern distractions to take their eyes off the mark. They pay too much attention to the things that don't matter and allow the things that matter to suffer," he began.

"I think you are right, sir," I said, grinning coyly, because I thought I had a share in the culpable verdict he passed regarding youth. I recalled how tempted I felt sometimes when I almost caved in for some peer pressure. I also remembered how *Oyinbo* and a number of other classmates took their eyes off the target and wasted what could have been their own humble beginnings.

"Many youths are more concerned with boyfriends and girlfriends these days than their future. They talk so much about dating and romance, even when they have no idea what those words truly mean." The banker shook his head slowly.

I could not fault anything he said. He was just blunt, telling me what many youths did not like to hear from adults. I was not in a haste to depart because the man had a lot to offer. I thought I should give him the chance to spill all of the advice that his own son rejected.

"Many kids disrespect their parents' opinions, and those of the other well-meaning adults in their lives, instead of listening to what they have to offer. Some children struggle for power with their teachers at school, as if that would yield something for them," he said.

"Well, they always realize how wrong they were in the end. Regrettably, it is sometimes too late by the time they get the message. There are no two ways to success. There are no shortcuts to it either, except taking the right paths...Making the right choices, hard work, perseverance, and standing up every time you fall."

The elderly man told me "the parable of the yam" decades ago, but I have held on to its life-changing lessons. I have told a number of young people who needed to hear the story. I advised them to take the right path to success. Fortunately, some of those who listened to the story changed their ways.

The bank manager's story remains relevant today, and more youths deserve to hear it, too. Modern youths face a lot of distractions: drugs and alcohol; peer-pressure; gangs; media; fashion; untimely dating; inappropriate role models; and the violence of the youths, by the youths, and for the youths; among other things that shouldn't take the front seats in their lives.

Dele Ajaja

Many youths spend more time on petty things at the expense of the things that matter. Wasting a lot of time at the make-up cabinet or discussing dating with friends for so long at the expense of better things is not a good way to start life. Spending a lot of time discussing trivial issues without doing school work is not advisable.

Scores of youths discard the priceless counsels by their parents and the other dependable adults in their lives. Instead, they embrace the badly thought-out alternatives offered by their poorly chosen friends and acquaintances. Some of the young people disrespect their teachers and engage in power struggle in the classroom instead of learning about things.

Others challenge authority simply because they want to get their peers' attention. They want other youths to see them as the only ones capable of challenging teachers and school authorities. Regrettably, they end up creating off-putting images of themselves and heading toward the wrong direction without realizing it.

Some youths waste precious time, expressing themselves in the wrong ways, long before grasping the fact that they took the wrong tracks. Some would be lucky if they turned a new leaf before it is too late. Regrettably, others may never find their feet again. The opportunities they need to succeed may never show up again, because some opportunities come only once.

The Hidden Treasures in Gray Hair

It is healthy for youths to express themselves and maintain their self-esteem, but there are good and bad ways to do this. For instance, calling unnecessary attention to oneself with constant disruption of the classroom is a bad way to express oneself. Being loud and unnecessarily cocky in the neighborhood is not a good way to show self-esteem.

Like the bank manager's story, it makes sense to be modest in the midst of peers instead of calling negative attention to oneself. It is rewarding to talk less when one has no meaningful things to say. Otherwise, one would present oneself as a silly fellow when one says ridiculous things, all in the name of getting attention.

There are good and bad ways to call attention to oneself. Like the tenacious yam, a young person could devote time to working hard at school, participating in sports, engaging in class activities, doing homework, studying habitually, making good grades, respecting teachers, showing regards to peers, participating in life-changing school and community clubs, and getting on the honor roll.

The above exercises are some of the appropriate ways to express and call positive attention to oneself, instead of disobeying teachers and the other authorities and getting appalling attention. Obviously, the youths who spend more time goofing around in the classroom than paying attention to their teachers hardly make good grades.

Dele Ajaja

Many youths pay more attention to video games than engaging in more gainful exercises. They spend a lot of hours sitting and watching musical videos than studying, doing homework, or participating in sports. They know more about celebrities than the current events in their communities, states, countries, or the world. It is healthy to play, but it should not be overtly more than necessary.

Some of the young people know more about recreational drugs than what is going on around the world. They misplace priorities by learning more about the inappropriate things than the appropriate ones. More than ever, younger generations are pushing to the background the values sought by older generations. Values like hard work, perseverance, respect, dignity, honesty, and the others are shrinking in society. Unfortunately, some adults sometimes enable the modern laissez-faire lifestyles.

Some youths prefer the gangs in their neighborhoods to the helpful youth clubs around them. They value life-destroying activities more than the advantageous behaviors. They accept the short-lived crooked rewards offered by gangs in place of the long-lasting beneficial rewards rendered by education. Gangs seem appealing to some young people, but gangs' destructive anecdotes are more than the thrills they offer.

Remember my grandmother's predictions? She said I would have as much food as I wanted

The Hidden Treasures in Gray Hair

someday, and I would even give to those who don't have something to eat. She said I would have that much if I kept going to school. It is necessary for me to mention that her forecast has come to pass. Now, I can eat as much as I want, and even give to those who have nothing to eat.

You'll also recall that I started out walking to school barefooted, and I did not have a jacket to keep myself warm when it was cold. Now, I can buy many shoes and wear as many suitable clothes as I want. I am grateful that I now live in my own comfortable house. All of these came to pass because I stayed in school. They also happened because I listened and learned from the responsible adults in my life.

Let me add that young people should not be distressed if the boys they want as boyfriends reject them, or the girls they want as girlfriends turn them down. It happened to me, too. However, I knew it was a matter of time—they would come back to me. They wanted me after I worked hard and gained admission into college. However, it was too late for them, because better ladies were already "eyeing" me. Youths should not feel sad because of the present, but instead work hard for a better future.

It is possible for one to overcome challenges and become successful in life. Acquisition of education is the contemporary prerequisite for accomplishment. I refrained from dropping out of school in spite of the challenges I faced as a child. I did not embrace the *"sagging"* of pants and wearing of gang bandanas as the ways to express myself. I rejected disruptive behaviors as forms of expression. Rather, I tried to express myself in positive manners. I did not look up to making money through drug dealing, but instead to acquiring education and the wisdom to move on in life.

Chapter 2
WISDOM—The Gift of a Lifetime

Lack of wisdom ravages a man more than a disease. A serious disease gives the patient a second chance if it is well managed, but lack of wisdom devastates the ignorant throughout his lifetime.

The *harmattan* was cold, but it was not potent enough to stop children from doing their morning chores. Scantily clad kids swept yards, fetched water from the brook, and carried trash to the dumpster. They stopped in their tracks occasionally, with their arms folded across their chests, and commented on the wintry and hazy weather of the month of December.

Remarks like, "Gee, it is cold today!" came out of their flapping mouths.

The children did not expect monetary allowances for what they did. They thought they should contribute something to their families' well-being, as their parents did more to make life better for them. However, the kids expected their parents to buy them clothes or shoes to celebrate the beginning of the New Year.

The young folks welcomed whatever offered them fun as they performed their tasks. Many amused themselves by singing and imploring *lekeleke*, the white-plumage cattle egrets that flew by, to paint their fingernails white. The children would lift and wave their hands as they sang, expecting the birds to paint their nails magically:

> *Lekeleke, adorn my nails with white*
> *Adaba bird, paint my nails white*
> *Lekeleke, adorn my nails with white*
> *Adaba bird, paint my nails white*

Flocks of the migratory egrets arrived during the *harmattan,* pecking the pests that irritated the cattle. The cattle did not protest when the birds perched on them, because the symbiotic relationship was mutually beneficial to the two creatures. The birds fed on the ticks that gnawed the cattle, and also warned them when unwanted guests approached. The egrets' spear-like beaks and tinning long legs differentiated them from local birds.

Shortly, the children would stop waving at the *lekeleke* and inspect their fingernails for white spots. Truly, some of them would find white tinges on their fingernails! Full of excitement, they would show their nails to one another, to confirm that the white spots were real.

The Hidden Treasures in Gray Hair

"Whoa! *Lekeleke* has painted my nails white," they would exclaim in amazement, believing that the birds actually granted their childish requests. The kids would have seen the white specks on their nails if they had inspected them before asking the birds to paint them. On the other hand, the adults knew that the white spots were on the children's nails before the latter asked the egrets to paint them.

The white spots on the nails could have occurred due to nutritional deficiencies, but the kids believed otherwise. They were smart in their own ways but lacking the wisdom to look at the larger picture before believing that the birds painted their nails magically. Many things appear like this to children around the world. The outward appearances of things fascinate them more than the other issues that surround those objects.

Children are children anywhere. They are spontaneous, innocent, and inadvertently naïve. They see the plain, harmless, and sparkling sides of life, without taking its complex sides into consideration immediately. Children are not dim-witted for being ordinary at that stage; it is simply a part of the developmental stages they have to go through. Thus, children need the counsel, support, and guidance of responsible elders as they grow.

The following analogy would illustrate the point more vividly. For a young person, life is like leaving a small town and going to the huge city of New York for the first time. Just as unanticipated road intersections confuse strangers, the youth who goes to the massive city alone would face a lot of challenges. However, the youth who goes with a responsible adult who knows New York City very well would have fewer problems.

As an adult, I experienced some challenges when I visited New York City for the first time. I was by myself, but the difference was that I engaged the experiences I'd gained during my previous sojourn in big cities. I anticipated the challenges I faced, and I had ideas about how to tackle them. I was familiar with the characteristics of the people in large cities. I knew the types of questions to ask, and the right people to pose those questions to. It was not a torturous experience, compared to what a lonely child could have encountered.

Experience matters in life. Whoever passes through a slippery alley and trips once is expected to be careful when passing through that path again. The person could even avoid that trail entirely and take another route. His previous downbeat experience would remain indelible in his memory, and he would not allow the same calamity to creep into his life again.

Adults have been around longer than youths, and the former have witnessed a lot of things during their lifetimes. Adults do things in certain ways or change how they do them, based on their past experiences. Young people should understand that good parents have reasons for asking them to do things in certain ways. The experiences acquired by the adults over the years offered them the wisdom to do things in those ways.

Wisdom is the capability to make sound judgments and prudent decisions. It means having the aptitude to identify the right actions and the best time to carry them out. It is the ability to decide on the appropriate words and knowing the right time to say them. Wisdom also involves the skill to envisage the outcomes of events. It is acquired with experience, persistence, understanding, shrewdness, patience, and of course, humility.

Generally, adults have more wisdom because of the scores of events and circumstances they have witnessed. The youths who pay attention to what insightful adults offer learn a lot and avoid making costly mistakes as they grow up. Giving an ear to the priceless suggestions made by reliable adults is not a waste of one's time. Such suggestions could be worth their weight in gold.

Listening to my grandparents (my mother's parents) was profitable to me. I learned a lot of wisdom from them before they were interred by Mother Earth. I discovered early that they had a lot to offer, and I had a lot to learn from them. I couldn't have allowed them to go into their graves with those golden words of wisdom locked away. The wisdom they passed on to me remains relevant today and it will be tomorrow.

"Save for the rainy day," Grandma told me many times. She taught me how to save money for the first time in my life. She insisted that I shouldn't spend all of my money at once, and I shouldn't be a compulsive buyer. She observed that I couldn't wait to spend the coins inside the clay piggy bank she bought for me as I became older. I kept the coins that visitors and relatives I ran errands for gave me in the piggy bank.

Grandma explained the wisdom behind saving for the rainy day. "You cannot spend all of your money on consumables like *pekere*," she said. She knew that I liked the fried corn paste in the morning and I spent much of my money on it.

"Those who spend their money carelessly don't have enough left for the day they really need money. You won't be able to save enough to buy something durable if you spend impulsively," Grandma counseled. I learned my lesson when a few peers who were patient and able to save, bought balls, colorful yo-yos, sunglasses, and other enviable accessories at the end of the year. I wished I had been prudent with my own money.

"I wish I saved some of the money I spent on *pekere*," I lamented. "I didn't need all of the oily snacks, after all." Thereafter, I felt like a graduate of a money-managing college. I even taught some of my peers how to "save for the rainy day," based on the wisdom I learned from my grandmother.

Grandma knew everything, I assumed, after I witnessed many of her words of advice coming to pass with reckonable precision. She once advised my older cousin, "the tailor apprentice," who had just completed learning how to sew cloth. My

The Hidden Treasures in Gray Hair

cousin was about to buy a used sewing machine from someone, but Grandma advised her to have a more experienced tailor inspect the machine before buying it.

"Don't rush to buy a fowl at the marketplace," began Grandma. "Its owner won't offer it for sale if it is capable of laying twenty eggs and hatching all of them to chicks," she warned. Grandma advised my cousin that the machine owner probably offered it for sale because it was giving her a problem.

Regrettably, my cousin bought the "shining" machine on her own, without having it inspected by a seasoned tailor.

"Whoever tries to collect rainwater with a basket deceives herself," Grandma said when she found out that my cousin bought the untested machine against her advice.

Grandma told you so, I thought, when my cousin started complaining a few weeks later, that every needle she fixed into the machine broke within minutes of working on a garment. She spent much of the money she charged her customers on buying needles instead of keeping the money as profit.

"Please, take Grandma's wisdom seriously the next time she tells you something," I advised my cousin.

Grandpa had a lot of wisdom, too. He gave suitable advice to everyone at every occasion. His words were some of the most profitable counsels that I heard as a young person. They remain alive and relevant today. I often apply them, and they have not failed me once.

A relative was not pleased that a policeman had arrested him at dusk because his bicycle did not have a light. He alleged that the policeman arrested him because they competed for a girlfriend years ago, and the policeman lost the competition. Grandpa noticed that the policeman could have been overzealous, but he agreed that people shouldn't ride their bikes without lights when it was dark.

"So, you knew that the aggrieved policeman was out there? Next time, don't take a shower with gasoline when someone is trying to set you on fire," Grandpa counseled the young man.

"I shouldn't have gone to that part of the town," the man agreed. "That's where the policeman patrols."

"Whoever wears white garment doesn't go to the stall where they sell palm oil," Grandpa said. I wished I knew many words of wisdom like my grandfather.

"I intend to join the police. I'll take that policeman to task when I become a police officer, too… Perhaps, I should go back and let him know how upset I am right now," the angry man fumed.

"Not so fast. Wait till you become a police officer. The child does not seek to punish the person who killed his father till he has a sword to fight with." My grandfather gave the man more words

The Hidden Treasures in Gray Hair

of wisdom to think about. The man understood my grandfather's advice. He thanked Grandpa as he departed.

"Take it easy, young man," Grandpa said. "It is he who dissects the ant carefully who sees its entrails. The ant's bowel is too minute to cut through hurriedly."

That day, I learned that people shouldn't place themselves in jeopardy when others were watching what they did. I also learned that people shouldn't say incriminating things when others were listening to them.

Grandpa was a successful farmer, but he wasn't a wealthy man. I suspected that he became a high-ranking chief because of his wisdom. They invited him to important town's meetings, and he was there whenever a dignitary visited the town. His wisdom fascinated me so much that I wanted to have some, too.

"Can you teach me wisdom, Grandpa?" I asked him one day, as we trekked to the farm. As an adolescent, I was most fascinated by my grandfather's insight. The elderly man hesitated. His face did not look like that of a man who couldn't answer a boy's question. Rather, he appeared like someone who had a lot to say, but was thinking of where to start from.

"Am I wise enough to teach you wisdom?" he inquired jovially as he glanced at me lovingly. "Wisdom is relative. It doesn't end with solving the riddle of whether the chick came before the egg or the egg came before the chick. It is also about making good to triumph over evil; the truth over a lie; humility over pride; and putting smiles on people's faces.

"Wisdom can sometimes be as simple as getting water out of a soaked sponge, and it can be as tricky as trying to squeeze water out of a rock sometimes. It has to do with bringing solution, succor, and justice to the people when they need them," he said. Grandpa thought he had not satisfied my yearning for an answer, so he continued with his explanations.

"Sometimes, wisdom is like an issue that puts honey in one's mouth and releases a foul-smelling gas from the anus at the same time. You want to swallow the sweet honey, yet you don't want to inhale the smelling gas," he went on. I couldn't resist my grandfather's teaching.

"Thank you, Grandpa, you are teaching me wisdom already," I said in appreciation of the beautiful expressions from him. I was glad that the farm was still far away, and Grandpa had a lot of time to teach me everything he wanted. He was the best counselor ever.

"It takes the person with wisdom to swallow the sweet honey and tolerate the smell that comes with farting at the same time," he said. "Life is full of pleasant and unpleasant experiences. It is he who has wisdom who is able to reconcile the extremes and come out smiling. That's what wisdom is all about.

The Hidden Treasures in Gray Hair

"Those who have wisdom don't say a lot when they are angry. They put some thought into what they say if they must talk. They don't say something simply because everyone is saying something. They wait till they have something real to say.

"Someone with wisdom understands when something doesn't turn out the way he or she wants—even after trying so hard. Whoever has wisdom knows when to let go. The ants bite the person who picks the palm-nuts (the ants' source of food). But, the ants let go and stop defending the palm-nuts when the picker puts the nuts on fire. Someone with wisdom understands that the divine admonishes whom it chooses. Providence dispenses life as it deems. Sometimes it sustains, and sometimes it overrules one's efforts."

"Will I ever have vast wisdom like you, Grandpa?" I asked.

"Why wouldn't you? The adult may be taller than the child now, but the child will catch up with the adult in the future," Grandpa said enthusiastically. "You could even have more wisdom than I have right now. After all, what appears like wisdom right now may look like foolishness in the future."

The remaining part of the journey to the farm was unusually pleasant as Grandpa told me a folktale that focused on wisdom. It was about how the tortoise, a supposedly insignificant animal, used wisdom to resolve the circumstance that endangered all animals.

Adults devised folktales using humans, animals, objects, and abstract things for educating and explaining complex subjects to children. That was especially useful when there were no formal schools many years ago. Folktales were used for teaching morals, life lessons, admonishment, and encouragement. Folktales were also used for entertainment by the moonlight.

Once upon a time, long before humans came into being, there was the animal kingdom.

"All animals must coexist peacefully, without some abusing the others," proclaimed *Olorun*, the creator of the heaven (and the earth). All of the animals followed the rules initially, as they lived happily with one another. There was absolute peace in the animal kingdom.

Unfortunately, the harmony in the kingdom started waning when the lion was inordinately possessed by pride. All animals honored him as the king of the jungle because of his strength, but he did not reciprocate the other animals' gestures.

"I don't have to respect the other animals," said the lion. "After all, I'm the most powerful animal in the kingdom." He was bossy, rude, and loud to everyone. The lion roared and forced other animals to comply with his overbearing wishes.

The uncouth king of the jungle started sitting at the head chair at every occasion even when he was not invited. Most animals were not happy about the development, but the other powerful animals, including the elephant, tiger, jaguar, cheetah, leopard, lynx, and caracal did not do anything. That was because the lion did not bother them and their families.

One day, the lion called a meeting of all the animals. "Send one of you to my den by sunrise every day," he ordered. "The designated animal will be my meal for that day. I will make the forest miserable for all of you the day I don't find an animal at my gate," he boasted.

The animals complied with the king's command for some time, but some became agitated after a while. "I'll die fighting, instead of making myself an easy prey for the overbearing lion," protested the monkey.

"The humiliation is too much!" mouthed the goat. "The strong animals that raise no fingers as a marauder terrifies their neighbors are not strong after all," he said about the elephant and the other influential animals that did nothing as the lion mortified the lower animals. The goat ran to the lion's den for a fight so he could regain his honor, but he did not return.

"Why would the tallest animal in the jungle tolerate the lion's cruelty against all animals?" questioned the giraffe. He went to the lion's den to fight with him. The lion heard his clattering hooves from afar and waited outside the den. He killed and ate the giraffe instantly. Other animals went, too. The footprints of all the animals that went to the lion's den faced that direction. None of them faced outward. The lion killed and ate them all.

All the animals became disillusioned as they had no way to deal with the rampaging lion. The animals' medicine man was at a loss over the issue, as all of his hypnotization and incantations did not work against the lion. The animals even sent emissaries to the other kingdoms for help.

Something unusual happened as the animals were about to give up hope for their freedom. Tortoise, the slow and strange animal that lived at the edge of the forest, offered to counter the lion. "There has been too much anger, but little wisdom," suggested the tortoise. "Anger cannot secure our honor from the lion, but wisdom can."

The other animals attempted to shout the tortoise down. "Who do you think you are? Are you *Ojogbon Eranko*, the all-knowing animal?" ridiculed the wolf. The scornful wolf started laughing and howling till the moon, the heavenly light, started shining fully, so it could see the entertaining wolf.

"Someone is seeking a moment of fame here," suggested the wolf. "Aren't you seeking fame, Tortoise? What can a lightweight animal like you do to the lion? The shrub that fails to bear someone's weight when he rests on it cannot kill that person if it falls on him. You cannot stop the lion."

The other animals were scornful of tortoise's daring move. They could not imagine the slow animal talking about tackling the fast lion when

The Hidden Treasures in Gray Hair

bigger animals had failed. The tortoise refrained from getting into a noisy match with his detractors. He thought it was unwise to fight with mouthy fellows in the dark. The mouthy fellows could be hailing themselves as the better fighters when one is pummeling them, because nobody sees what is going on in the dark.

"I understand your concern about my size and slow nature, when the bigger and swifter animals cannot kill the lion. It doesn't matter who kills the lion now. It doesn't matter if a man sees a venomous snake, and a woman kills it. What matters is for the dangerous snake not to escape. I will fight the lion and get the animals' honor back," the unruffled tortoise offered.

The other animals burst into uncontrollable laughter, as they thought the tortoise was possessed by some drunken demons. The jackal laughed till he became dehydrated because he lost much of the water in his body as tears through his eyes. The anteater was so amused that he opened his mouth till ants started crawling into it.

"I do not seek fame at the most critical period in the lives of all animals," explained the tortoise. "Whoever seeks fame by fighting the dangerous lion will die and lose everything anyway." He tried further to sell his plan to humble the discourteous lion.

"Stop goofing around, Tortoise, nobody is kidding around here. Something serious is going on in the animal kingdom. How do you fight the king of the jungle when you don't even have fearful claws?" questioned the ostrich. The tortoise refused to argue with the ostrich. He knew the ostrich as the flightless bird who buried his head in the sand whenever there was a problem and pretended that nobody saw him.

"I hereby challenge the lion to a fight at the town's square in three days. The king of the jungle should kill and eat me, if he wins. Otherwise, he should humble himself and stop killing the other animals!" The tortoise requested with a tone of finality. As expected, the lion's informants went to tell him about the slow animal's confrontation.

"A piece of cake!" exclaimed the lion. "Think of a special recipe for cooking the tortoise. He will become a good meal for me in three days' time," he told his chef.

The town's square was alive in three days' time with mischievous animals who wanted to witness the lion kill and eat the tortoise. The best drummers among the animals hit the drums powerfully, and the singers went wild with songs that made fun of the tortoise:

The tortoise rams the king
He rams the king
The king is not ached
He rams the king

The slow fellow defies the king
He defies the king
The king is not defied
He defies the king

The Hidden Treasures in Gray Hair

The tortoise dares the king
He dares the king
It's about dinner time
Here's another meal for the king

"The contempt toward honey does not take away from its sweetness. It is he who cuts the tree branch who wastes his time; the tree will sprout again." The tortoise did not take the naughty song against him seriously.

Prior to the fight, the tortoise went to the forest to fill the three gourds with which he planned to fight the lion. He filled them with three colored fluids. The other animals were not aware of that, but they saw him bringing the gourds to the town square. Of course, they did not know their contents. The tortoise was also slippery with the slimy okra paste he'd rubbed all over himself. None of the animals applauded because they saw the tortoise as the loser, even before the fight started.

On the other hand, the animals went berserk when the lion approached the town square in grandeur. His eyes were crimson-red like blood, and his mane stood like irritated cobras. The lion's tail shot like an angry arrow. All animals departed from the lion's path as if pushed by tons of powerful waves from the ocean.

"Hail the king! Hail the king! Hail the king!" the lion's *yes-men* yelled.

The lion surged ahead and tried to grab the tortoise, but the smaller animal slipped away effortlessly from his grips. The slippery okra on the tortoise's body was working as intended.

"It is neither by force nor by muscle, but by wisdom," whispered the tortoise as he thought about his next move. The lion surged forward at that time, trying to grab the tortoise the second time. Surprisingly, the slippery animal slipped away from the lion again.

"How possible is that?" asked some of the animals, as they watched the tortoise giving the king of the jungle a hard time. It appeared like the impossible was becoming possible. Some animals started thinking about the possibility that all, except the divine, was invincible, after all.

The lion was so frustrated and angry. He jumped as high as he could, hoping to pin his opponent to the ground. Tortoise, the brainy animal, ducked quickly. The lion broke his neck as he landed on his own head.

The tortoise quickly carried one of the three gourds and smashed it on the lion's body. The red solution inside spilled on the lion like blood. The tortoise smashed the second gourd on the lion's nose, and its slimy contents dripped as if the lion was discharging mucous from his nostril. The lion started groaning as the pains in his broken neck advanced.

All of the animals were amazed. Adding more to the amazement, the tortoise smashed the third

The Hidden Treasures in Gray Hair

gourd on the lion's head. The gray matter inside smeared the lion's head as if his brain was coming out.

The surprised animals ran from one end of the forest to the other, celebrating the downfall of the cruel king of the jungle. As far as the animals could see, they thought the tortoise beat the lion till blood started coming out of his body. They believed that he clobbered the king of the jungle and mucous came out of his nose. The animals also assumed that the tortoise bashed the lion's head and part of his brain came out.

The helpless lion could not bear the pains. Above all, he could not face the other animals as he was so shameful. He simply covered his face with his large paws and winced with pains. The animals carried the tortoise shoulder-high and sang his praise as the lion's *yes-men* walked away.

The drummers and singers changed everything in favor of tortoise, the slow animal they'd made fun of earlier:

Behold the new star in the sky
Tortoise! A new star was born today
The fighting luminary of our time
Tortoise! A new star was born today
One of its kinds in an era
Tortoise! A new star was born today

What comes before downfall?
Pride comes before fall
Watch the lion wincing

Pride comes before fall
Watch arrogance groaning
Pride comes before fall.
"Power, might, and muscle do not solve all of the world's problems. Navigating the tricky waterways of life requires wisdom and good character," concluded Grandpa as the hut at *Oke-Ona*, his far-away farm, came to sight.

Chapter 3
CHARACTER—The Authentic Beauty

Character is the real beauty of a person. A good-looking individual without character is like an exhibition mannequin that appears full on the outside but is filled with emptiness inside.

"All stand! Greet," requested the class captain as the teacher walked into the classroom. The teacher was usually the last person to enter the classroom. Students sang and marched to the classroom from the morning assembly, and the teacher followed a moment later.

Arriving after the teacher was not an option, except when a student had a very good excuse. Schools observed the order of precedence. They taught the youth that it was disrespectful for the subordinates to arrive late after the higher-ranking individuals had arrived promptly.

"Good morning, Ma!" the students responded in unison as they stood to acknowledge the teacher.

"Good morning, students. Please, have your seat," replied the teacher as she walked gracefully to her desk.

"Present, Ma," answered each of the students as the teacher took the attendance. The classroom remained serene and orderly because students knew it was discourteous to act otherwise in front of the teacher. People treated tutors like mini-gods across the region.

Students and their parents respected educators a lot. They couldn't think of more deserving humans than the teachers, "who turned hard heads to soft ones." They believed that no one created a better community than those who taught people how to read, put pen to paper, and comprehend the tricks of Mother Nature.

Students were not only respectful; they worked very hard, too. Each of them cut a portion of the grass on campus with *oj'agba*, the slim metal blade. They picked trash on campus frequently. The mud-walled latrines (restrooms) and the other parts of the campus were clean. The students watched out for whoever trashed the campus because they cleaned everywhere themselves. There was no graffiti on the walls either. The students were careful not to dirty the school so that they would not have to do additional cleaning.

The Hidden Treasures in Gray Hair

Teachers were not rich, but they had it so good. Local students showed their gratitude by stopping at teachers' houses and bringing their bags and briefcases to school in the morning. They repeated the same task when school closed. Sometimes, students voluntarily cleaned teachers' houses or worked at their farms on weekends, even when the latter did not ask for help. Parents encouraged their children to be thankful to their teachers.

Above all, teachers did not have to follow students everywhere. The latter typically behaved well when adults were not around. They understood the consequences of fighting or violating other school rules and regulations. The students believed they would misrepresent their families' values if they misbehaved at school, and their parents would be upset at them.

The "class captains" or "class monitors," who were students themselves, made sure their classmates behaved well when teachers were not around. The student-leaders played the supervision role whenever the youths were on their own. There was never a long phase of leadership vacuum among the students.

That was school back then. The general level of discipline reflected in students' progress. They did their homework promptly, participated in class activities and sports. Resultantly, most students did well academically. Coming late to school, ditching, lack of respect, disruptive behaviors, littering, and the other violations were rare, because the infractions came with firm consequences. Students preferred to follow the rules than take some lashes of the cane or cut grasses with *oj'agba*.

❖ ❖ ❖

The level of discipline was high at the local high school. All students understood why they should follow the rules and regulations. They knew why they had to respect those in positions of authority. Baba Olaoba, the principal, spoke about character so much that no one could resist it.

"Character is your inner beauty. It is the key to the door of success in life," he explained. Everyone understood how serious the head teacher was whenever he moved around the platform with his hands folded behind him. That was the man's idiosyncrasy that nobody misinterpreted.

"Your external beauty is in vain if you lack inner beauty. Real people judge you by your moral quality more than your physical beauty," admonished the man whom students and teachers regarded as the principal of principals. He was truly an all-time role-model—a disciplined, dedicated, and hard-working man who cared a lot about his students.

The role of character in judging people was preached everywhere. There were no hiding places for unruly youths. Students would do anything to avoid being sucked into the hole called the School Board Disciplinary Committee. The board passed words round whenever schools expelled students for serious offenses. Such students usually had a hard time when they tried to re-enroll elsewhere.

I transferred to another school midway through the high school. The change had nothing to do with my character. My father wanted me to move to another town so I could have diverse views of the world. People believed that those who moved around learned more about life than those who were stationary. I was not surprised when my new principal started talking about character, too.

"Each of you design your testimonial every day," began Chief Ayeleso at the morning assembly. "Your teacher only writes on paper whatever you design for yourself," he added. All eyes were on the principal every time he spoke about testimonials because no student wanted a bad one.

Students received "testimonials" in addition to their academic certificates when they graduated from the high school. The testimonial looked like a certificate, but it contained statements about the student's character, level of cooperation with staff and peers, and participation in extracurricular activities.

Students needed good academic certificates as well as acceptable testimonials to move on to higher institutions or career paths. Some graduating students who were good academically, but lacked good character, had some problems. On the other hand, those who were average academically, but had good character, did not have such problems. That was another way the authority devised to infuse character in young people.

"Your parents and teachers are doing all they could for you to have good character. However, your capacity to acquire good moral fiber depends on you." Chief Ayeleso said at the morning assemblies.

Mr. Ogundana, the boardinghouse master and geography teacher, was equally passionate about character. He was not a run-off-the-mill teacher. The students thought of him as a teacher of teachers—a candid, disciplined, and hardworking man who minced no words when it came to telling things as they were.

"Everyone you address as 'Sir' or 'Ma' appreciates it, but it doesn't cost you a penny to say so," remarked the boardinghouse master. "You earn kindness from those you say respectful words to, but you don't labor to say those words. You have nothing to lose when you have good character."

The talks about character were so strong that people accepted morality as the wind beneath people's wings. They believed that morality gave people a thrust when they needed a push. Everyone spoke about how good nature elevated people and bad nature demoted people. The populace believed that those who had the good things of life, but lacked character, did not have it all.

Every adult was involved in training the young people. The task of imparting character to the youth was the responsibility of all. It was common

The Hidden Treasures in Gray Hair

for a "stranger" to admonish an offending youth he met in the street for the first time. Every adult acted like a parent when the biological parents were not around. Thus the saying, "It takes the whole village to raise a child."

People did what was expected of them when nobody was watching. They believed that someone was observing them from above. For example, farmers did not have to stand at the roadside and watch the produce they had for sale. They would arrange them on stalls along the road, and signified their prices with the number of rocks next to them.

People were trustworthy. It was unusual for passersby to steal from the stalls, because they placed character before personal cravings. However, a youth went against the wisdom of good character that day. We were returning from the farm when we saw two teenagers arguing near a farmer's stall. One of them carried a bunch of bananas, and the other attempted to convince him to return the fruits or pay for them.

"People with character don't take what belongs to others, simply because the owners are not watching," counseled the conscientious youth. "The king of heaven sees you if the king of earth doesn't."

"I don't care about the king of heaven right now. People have to enjoy themselves here on earth before going to answer the king of heaven," the offending youth responded sarcastically.

He attempted to move away, but the other youth heaved him toward the farmer's stall.

"You'll care about the king of heaven when I report you to your father," cut in my grandmother. "Are you not the son of the hunter who lives around the corner from my house?" Many criminal-minded individuals were deterred because people interacted and knew one another's family in the town. The physical features of a youth could indicate who his parents were.

"Please, don't involve my father in this. I'll return the bananas," surrendered the fleeing young man. "I pledge to be of good character henceforth," he promised as he returned the fruits to the stall. The youth was clearly embarrassed, and his newly found demeanor revealed that he meant what he said.

Everyone was expected to engage the golden rule when dealing with others. The tenets of decency, integrity, respect, hard work, courage, fairness, dependability, kindness, and loyalty were emphasized at different forums. Hardly a day passed without an adult talking about the system of belief. The youths, too, reminded their peers who fell short of the ideals to behave appropriately.

The adults often engaged folktales for advocating good character. Morality was the theme of the stories engaged for such purpose. One of the stories told at schools was about the consequence of losing touch with morality. The story

The Hidden Treasures in Gray Hair

also centered on *Ijapa Tiroko*, the crafty tortoise that showed up in many Yoruba folktales.

Once upon a time, when animals lived with humans and talked like them, there was an animal that lacked good character. The tortoise was greedy and never thanked others for what they did for him. The insatiable animal would do anything to cheat, including lying and harassing others.

Conversely, the king of that town was kind and generous. He demonstrated charity by being truthful, caring, and sharing with his subjects. No one was surprised when the king invited the people to eat at his palace during a famine. He invited his subjects every day, and saved many who would have starved to death.

There was famine because rain did not fall for a long time. The sun scorched the earth and there was poor harvest in the whole region. Grains were scarce and the available quantities were too expensive for ordinary people to buy. Everyone was heartbroken and afraid that the hard times might linger.

"My precious subjects, I could feel your frustrations, hunger, and anger at this difficult moment in our town's history," said the king. "But I assure you that the sufferings will not last. The divine will hear our prayers and dispense rain on our fields. Our crops will grow and our children will feed well again."

Everyone in the village except the tortoise appreciated the king's kindness. The people loved the king, but the tortoise was jealous of him. He wished he was the one inviting people to dine at his house every day, but he lacked the resources to do so. The tortoise started coveting the king's good fortune and fame.

The monarch was able to feed the people with the magical wand bequeathed him by his deceased father. The king would hit the magical stick on the ground once and request food. He could ask for whatever foods he wanted and assorted foods would appear. Then, all of his guests would feast and even take food home for the rest of the day.

The tortoise was not happy that he could not feed people at his house like the king. He decided to take the magical wand from the king. The covetous animal thought about different diabolical ways he could achieve his plan, but couldn't settle for one immediately.

"I will trick the king and take his magical wand," thought the tortoise in the evening. "Then, my family will become the most famous in the land." The tortoise did not sleep the whole night. He was thinking about the plan to relieve the king of his supernatural wand.

"I got it!" cried the tortoise in the middle of the night. His startled wife asked for an explanation for the sudden noise, but the trickster responded sloppily.

The Hidden Treasures in Gray Hair

"Don't worry, *Yannibo*, my dear, we'll talk about it in the morning," retorted the tortoise.

The tortoise knew that the king's daughter bathed at the river next to his farm every morning. The cunning animal knew how inquisitive and playful the princess was, and he wanted to take advantage of those characteristics. Tortoise's palm trees did not do well because of the harsh weather, but one of the trees grew a single palm kernel.

The tortoise went to his farm early in the morning, before the king's daughter arrived for her morning swimming. He climbed the palm tree as soon as the princess and her attendants approached the river. The tortoise waited as the princess prepared to enter the water. He quickly cut the single palm kernel and tossed it at the princess' feet.

"Wow! What a beautiful fruit," exclaimed the princess. "It is red as ruby, and smooth as a puzzling seed. I won't let it leave my sight." The king's daughter took the palm kernel with her into the water.

The tortoise was patient. He watched as the princess entered the water and started swimming. She began to play with the fruit as she splashed water. Suddenly, the smooth fruit slipped from the princess's grip and went downstream with the water current. The king's daughter and her attendants tried to retrieve the fast-moving palm kernel to no avail.

That was exactly what the tortoise wanted. His plan was working as perfectly as he wished. He climbed down the palm tree quickly and ran to the river bank. He wasted no time in confronting the princess about the fruit she took into the river.

"Where is my palm kernel, Princess Awelewa?" he asked. "Didn't you take it with you into the river moments ago?" The tortoise started panting and pretending that he was dead serious about the loss of his palm kernel.

"I'm deeply sorry, *Ijapa Tiroko oko Yannibo*," hailed the princess, hoping that her civility would calm the greedy animal. "The famous husband of *Yannibo*, I saw the fruit, but I didn't know it belonged to you."

"Where is my fruit, Princess? You are rich and spoiled, but I'm poor and broke. I need the single palm kernel more than anything. Everyone understands how tough life has become," the tortoise lamented.

"Again, I'm sorry, Tortoise. I entered the river with the palm kernel, but it slipped away from my grip as I swam. Please, my father would give you a bunch of palm kernels, if you want." The princess pleaded with the tortoise without knowing his motive.

"How many times do I have to repeat myself, Princess?" queried the tortoise. "I'm not a spoiled fellow. I don't need a bunch of palm kernels. I want my single fruit, the exact one you carelessly tossed into the river."

The Hidden Treasures in Gray Hair

The princess was confused. She did not know what to tell the tortoise again. Instead, she requested the animal to follow her to the palace to see her father, the king. She knew that her father would take care of the issue satisfactorily. The princess and her attendants led the way and the tortoise followed them to the palace.

"*Kabiyesi*, the unquestionable one," hailed the tortoise as he stood before the king. He wept profusely as he told his supposedly pitiable story. "O king! You are the merciful one, and the bearer of justice. The princess threw my only palm kernel into the river, and now I'm ruined, as I have nothing left under the sun.

"I went to my farm, beside the river, this morning, to harvest my only palm kernel. I planned to provide the last meal for my family before the famine kills us, but the princess deliberately threw the fruit away." The tortoise continued with his pathetic story.

The princess attempted to tell her innocent side of the story, but the tortoise would not listen. He started another round of crying and panting, pretending to be deeply touched by the loss of his palm kernel.

"Take it easy, Tortoise," counseled the king. "One palm kernel was not enough to prepare a meal for your family. What if I give you as many bunches of palm kernels as you want?"

"I appreciate your kind gesture, *Kabiyesi*, but I'm not a greedy fellow. I want nothing more than my single palm kernel. Precisely, I want the exact one that Princess Awelewa tossed in the river," the tortoise mandated. He knew that the town's bylaw said the victim had the right to ask for the exact thing the defendant took from the victim.

The king and his chiefs appealed to the tortoise to accept some bunches of palm kernels in place of his single fruit, since the river had carried away the latter. Everyone thought the tortoise was insane, but they had no idea what the cunning animal was up to.

"All right, Tortoise, ask for whatever you want," commanded the king. "I believe the river has carried away your palm kernel and you cannot have the exact one again." The gentle king was infuriated by the tortoise's irrational attitude. If only he understood what the animal's motive was, he would have said something different.

"Thank you, *Kabiyesi*," began the tortoise. "Everyone understands what our law says about the crime committed against someone. The victim dictates what he or she wants in that case. Please, understand that I'm not trying to be difficult. But I'm the victim, and..." He launched a long and winding expression.

"Are you willing to tell me what you want, *Ijapa*?!*"* bawled the king, who was infuriated by the tortoise's snaky rhetoric.

"All right, *Kabiyesi*. If it pleases your honor, I want your magical wand," the sly tortoise said at last.

The Hidden Treasures in Gray Hair

"I understand your loss, Tortoise, but can't you let me pay you a lump sum of money? You know how precious the wand is to me. By the way, I use it for feeding the people at this time of big famine," the king pleaded with the tortoise.

"You know what I want, *Kabiyesi*. I would have asked for money if I were a greedy fellow. I want the magical wand." The tortoise repeated the restitution he wanted.

The monarch and his chiefs got the message. The victim had the moment whenever someone offended another person. The king had no option than to give the mystical wand to the cunning animal.

"Have your way, *Ijapa*. Here's the wand," the monarch said and offered the tortoise the wand.

The fraudulent tortoise returned home like a valiant fellow, as he hired drummers and singers to accompany him. He thanked those who followed him home and locked the door tightly behind him. First of all, the tortoise tested the magical wand by hitting it on the ground once and asking for a variety of foods. The whole house was instantly full of assorted foods and exotic wines.

The tortoise and his family ate and drank as much as they could and partied all night. The following day, they invited their friends, neighbors, acquaintances, and celebrities to celebrate with them. The tortoise did not hit the magical wand on the ground before his guests arrived. He wanted to demonstrate his newly found prowess in their presence. Besides, he wanted the visitors to eat and drink fresh foods and wines.

Many people, including *Ijapa's* and *Yannibo's* extended families, friends, acquaintances, and the famous people in the town, arrived at the tortoise's house. The family was surprised to see the faces of long-lost friends who had stopped talking to them many years before. They even saw people they barely knew, who now acted like long-time jolly friends.

The mood was incomparable to anything that Ijapa and his wife had witnessed in their lives. They were so pleased to be the center of attraction at such gathering. More people arrived shortly and Ijapa's yard was not large enough to occupy the people. The guests started spilling into Ijapa's neighbors' yards.

"Welcome, fellow citizens of *Fair-Weather* town. Of course, you are not fair-weather friends. You came here because you care about me and my humble family. As all of you may have noticed, I have worked diligently all of my life, and now I'm getting something back for those years of wealth building." The cunning tortoise really wanted to eulogize himself and his bogus prosperity.

The tortoise had no real success story to tell, but he managed to pull a fast one on his brand-new whatever-goes friends. The fair-weather guests did not mind tortoise's off-putting speech. They even clapped, whistled, and roared for the verbose statements.

The Hidden Treasures in Gray Hair

"My dear friends, it is my pleasure to welcome you to diverse dishes and exotic wines from the four corners of the world," bragged the tortoise. He brought out the magical stick and hit it on the ground twice. Tortoise hit the wand twice, as opposed to once, because he wanted plenty of food for his large guests.

"I want different foods and wines from the different parts of the world," commanded the tortoise.

Unknown to him, the magical wand shouldn't be hit on the ground twice. The supernatural stick multiplied so fast immediately and started hitting tortoise, his family, and their guests, instead of supplying them with exotic foods and wines. The wands were very fast. They hit all of the people at the gathering before they could escape from that neighborhood.

The tortoise was full of sores as he ran. The sticks followed him and his family everywhere they went. They headed to the king's palace to seek refuge. The avaricious animal expected the caning to stop as soon as they arrived at the king's palace. He wanted to return the magical wand to the king.

"*Kabiyesi! Kabiyesi!! Kabiyesi!!!*" yelled the tortoise as he ran into the palace with the other members of his family at his heels. The sticks did not stop hitting them. "Please, rescue us, the rescuer of the helpless," *Ijapa* sobbed uncontrollably.

The king and the other members of the royal family came out and witnessed the magical wands hitting the tortoise and his family. Perhaps, more than the beating, the tortoise was full of shame as he begged the king to take back the wand. He sprawled on the ground and licked the princess's feet as the sticks hit him.

"Forgive me, Princess. I lied to you about the lone palm kernel. I set you up so I could take the king's magical wand. Please, plead with the king to stop the sticks from hitting me and my family," *Ijapa* kept talking as he sobbed.

"You asked for it, *Ijapa*. Now, you can have it," The king said and ordered the tortoise and his family out of the palace. The greedy animal, his wife, and children headed for the bush as the magical sticks hit them. Ever since, the tortoise and his family live in the bush, and their shells remain rough as a result of the beatings from the magical sticks.

Good character is the authentic beauty of a person. Whoever is blessed with physical beauty is not complete till the inner beauty complements the outer beauty. Engaging the golden rule when dealing with others is the best policy anyone could possess. Respect, understanding, and charity toward others set those who have them apart from those who lack them.

What happens when you throw a tennis ball at a concrete wall? The ball bounces back to you. The law of nature states that the rock that one

The Hidden Treasures in Gray Hair

throws up comes back down. In the same manner, people get back what they do to others. The farmer harvests the same crop he sows, as no one plants hot pepper and reaps sweet potato. Events have their own ways of catching up with those who lack good character. I encourage all youths to embrace good character and associate with the people who have good character, too.

Chapter 4
ASSOCIATION—The Defining Choice

The sheep that associates with dogs would eat what dogs eat. Your choice of friendship defines your personality. Whoever associates with law-breakers is perceived as a criminal.

Growing up in a poor home was daunting, but it came with its own silver lining. My grandparents' inability to buy noticeable toys for me boosted my creativity. I made my own playthings with available materials. I used local objects to make replicas of the toys owned by well-off children, and my fabrications worked satisfactorily well. However, I started earning a little money through manual labors as I grew older, so I could buy what I wanted.

The other children whose parents could not afford toys made their own, too. We all had fun without factory-made toys. Some of the things we made were simple, and some were fairly complex. *Okoto*, the spinning top, was very simple to make. I would go to nearby bush and pick lifeless miniature snails, then remove their remains with broomsticks. I would rub the shells' open ends on the concrete to make them even.

Thereafter, one or more players would join me to spin the shells on the ground. A player would hold a shell between his thumb and the middle finger, with the open end facing up, and spin it as fast as he could. He would allow it to whirl on the ground for a while. Then he would undercut its lower end with one or several fingers, so the shell's top could overturn and face the ground.

Okoto sometimes generated a lot of excitement and crowds. The players would sit on the ground, and the spectators would stand around them in a circle. The audience showed their enthusiasm by hailing each player with the song:

This kid has become okoto
He spins on his bottom
Round and round
He has become okoto
He spins on his bottom
Round and round

The player who failed to make the shell face the ground was the losing contestant. Losing the match came with a consequence. The unsuccessful player would allow the other player(s) to thump the back of his hand with the shell. The winning player would hold the lower end of the shell with

The Hidden Treasures in Gray Hair

his thumb and middle finger and propel it vigorously on the back of the losing player's hand.

Many of my peers and I sometimes built model cars and trucks with milk tins and discarded flip-flops. We made the windshields and windows with transparent bread wrappers. We even fabricated toys that moved on their own. We used tensioned rubber bands to generate motion in one of the parts, and the moving piece moved the other parts in turn.

Additionally, I enjoyed other activities with the kids in my neighborhood and the local school. We dug the watersides for crabs, and searched for mushrooms in the bushes. We kept tadpoles as pets in water containers, thinking they were small fishes. We took part in hide-and-seek games around the neighborhood. We listened to tales by the moonlight late in the evening. We also solved riddles.

"*Alo o,*" announced the one who had a riddle.

"*Alo-o-o!*" responded the enthusiastic kids.

"Who eats with the king without tidying the table thereafter?" asked the riddle presenter.

"I know the answer!" responded several kids who knew the response.

"What's the answer, *Oluwasola*?" asked the presenter.

"Housefly," responded the girl excitedly.

"You are right, *Oluwasola*!" commended the presenter.

A resounding applause followed the answer. Obviously, the housefly has no respect for anyone, including the king. The little fly would take a bite from anyone's food and depart without helping to tidy up the table.

The other children and I also engaged in sporting activities, including football (otherwise called soccer), running, and wrestling. *Ijakadi* or *udi*, the local parlances for wrestling, attracted large spectators, too. Two wrestlers would engage one another and the audience would sing till the back of a combatant touched the ground:

> *Lakiti is the better fighter*
> *He knows how to fight*
> *Lakiti is the better fighter*
> *He knows how to fight*
> *Attempt to twist him down*
> *He would uncoil smartly*
> *Lakiti is the better fighter*

I did not mind giving up anything, so I could enjoy my peers' company, and they would do the same for me, too. Some of us were inseparable. We ate from the same bowls and went about together. The adults understood how close we were, but they knew we could not be together forever.

"Twenty children don't play together for twenty years," the adults would reflect whenever some families moved. The adage did not mean much to me back then, because the departing families hardly moved far away. They only departed from family houses to their own, at short distances with-

The Hidden Treasures in Gray Hair

in the town. Unlike the adults, who had a lot to do, the children visited their peers frequently, regardless of where they relocated in the town.

Additionally, the children attended the same local school and saw one another regularly. I did not think so much of when some things would separate me from my peers. But the axiom that twenty children don't play together for twenty years started coming to pass as we grew older. Some kids left the town to learn some trades elsewhere. Also, one of my peers started exhibiting unusual behaviors, and some parents started warning their children to stop associating with him.

"The sheep that associates with dogs would eat what dogs eat," said my grandmother while warning me not to associate with Ade, a senior chief's son. People had been suspecting him for owning sophisticated toys, when his mother denied buying them for him. He claimed to have found the money with which he bought the toys along the road every time.

The adults did not believe that he found the money with which he bought expensive things so frequently, but the kids did not know the difference. We believed Ade's stories. We thought he was luckier than the rest of us every time he "found" money and bought a toy. I tried to defend him when Grandma warned me to stay away from him.

"He probably found the money with which he bought the toys from people's wallets, not along the road," suggested Grandma. "Besides, people were expected to look for the owners and return the monies they found instead of spending them anyhow they wanted."

I couldn't stomach the idea of parting ways with Ade, with whom I'd grown up in the neighborhood and attended the same school. I sometimes thought he was the victim of a conspiracy by the hard-to-please adults. "How could Ade become a bad boy after being good for so long?" I contemplated while thinking that most kids were not better than Ade.

"There are good kids around. You don't have to stick with the reckless kids, simply because you want to belong," my grandmother counseled, on noticing that I had difficulty parting ways with Ade. "You could look at the gentle face of the moon if it is difficult to look at the glaring face of the sun. You could look for trustworthy kids if your friends are becoming untrustworthy."

Ade was one or two years older than me. He was taller and slightly bigger, but we belonged to the same generation. We played together in the neighborhood and attended the same elementary school. We were even in the same grade. We stomped the puddles together in the streets. Ade was a sweet kid, but things started falling apart as we grew older.

Ade began to associate with suspicious youths. He started having more money than the

The Hidden Treasures in Gray Hair

boys of his age. He sometimes bought lunch for everyone who played with him. We marveled at his generosity without thinking of his source of income. We thought we were being fair to Ade, the generous kid.

Many kids appreciated Ade's generosity and were delighted to be his friend. After all, the one who shared with the less fortunate was considered the good-hearted person. We did not see anything wrong with our line of thinking, but the adults thought otherwise. Conscientiously, we thought we should not judge or become opinionated about another person.

I had an opportunity to revaluate Ade's innocence one afternoon on the way from school. He stopped at a retailer's kiosk and asked for something odd. I thought he was buying *Goody-Goody*, the chocolate candy fancied by most kids. Regrettably, Ade requested for something suspicious.

"Give me three sticks of *orange-butt* S.M," requested Ade. S and M were the initials for Sweet Menthol, a brand of cigarette that came in orange and white butts. That was the brand of cigarettes smoked by one of my distant uncles, who later died of cancer. I saw my uncle with packs of those cigarettes years before he died.

"May be Grandma was right about not associating with Ade," I told myself as Ade received his change from the retailer. Anyone who knew how generous Ade was should expect what happened next. He was the bighearted kid who shared everything with the people around him. There were three of us on the way home, and he bought three sticks of cigarettes.

"Here, take," Ade said, offering me a stick of cigarette. He was wrong for expecting me to accept it from him. Most kids viewed cigarette smoking by young people as strange, and I was one of them.

"No, I don't smoke!" I said with an expression of shock. I tried to tell Ade how disgusting it was to smoke cigarettes, but he called me names.

"You are just a local boy who has no idea what it takes to be sophisticated," Ade said.

"What about you, Elijah?" Ade offered the same stick of cigarette to the other kid. I was relieved when the boy looked at the cigarette, glanced at me, shrugged, and declined. Everyone was quiet momentarily, but we continued our journey shortly. Ade soon stopped at an alley and bid us goodbye.

I gave my grandmother's advice a serious thought as I trekked home. I thought that Ade, whom I'd stood by when others stood against, had crossed the line. For the first time in my life, I reflected on the adage that twenty children don't play together for twenty years. Although we lived in the same neighborhood, attended the same school, and were in the same grade, I thought it was time to part ways with Ade.

"The quality of friendships you make says a lot about you," counseled Grandma later when I

The Hidden Treasures in Gray Hair

reported to her what happened. "You don't have any business with Ade from now on. You knew that kids shouldn't smoke cigarettes."

"You know I won't smoke, Grandma, even if I associate with Ade," I tried to assure her of my determination to remain a good boy.

"You shouldn't associate with those who use illegal substances if you don't intend to use those substances," reasoned Grandma. "People are tempted to do illegal things when they associate with those who do them. Additionally, people assume that you do illegal things when you associate with those who do them. It could be erroneous, but people judge others based on whom they associate with."

I understood my grandmother's argument, and the events that followed proved her right. Ade did not show up at school for a while. Then, he reappeared one day with the scent of alcohol on his breath. I knew he was coming to the end of his academic career because schools did not give reckless students the chance to pollute the good ones.

Ade hissed for no reason as the teacher entered the classroom. Everyone knew there would be a problem if we failed to point out the disrespectful student. It was customary for the whole class to take the punishment if they covered up for the student who misbehaved.

"You better own up or I will point you out," I whispered to Ade. By this time I was fed up with his out-of-line demeanor. He motivated me to call out his name sooner by giving me a dirty look and the gesture that everyone understood as "I'll deal with you after school." I called out Ade's name to the teacher, and he received some consequences for his action.

In line with his threat, Ade punched me a number of times on the way home in the afternoon. I attempted to walk away, but the older and bigger boy only gave me more punches.

My grandmother took me to Ade's house on seeing the bruises on my face, but his family had no clue where he was. He possibly expected my grandmother to visit his home after the assault. Calling the police was out of the question as every family knew one another. It was unconventional to call police to one's neighbors back then.

Ade soon dropped out of school and joined the group of teenagers who bragged about being business people. The young merchants would disappear for weeks and reappeared with modest merchandise. However, people realized that they were spending more than the volume of their businesses. Girls flocked to them, and they were the toasts of the parties organized by the trendy youths in the town.

Ade and the other young "business people" out-dressed their peers. They wore expensive clothes and accessories. Their wristwatches and other jewelries were unmatched by those worn by the other youths. Clearly, they were making money from elsewhere, apart from the businesses they told people about.

Before long, words started filtering out through the grapevine that the young merchants were engaging in armed robbery in neighboring towns. Ade once returned from a journey with unexplained scars on his body. He claimed he was involved in an accident, but people disbelieved him after he changed stories several times.

There was little Ade's mother could do beyond talking to him. Ade stopped talking to her a few months after he turned eighteen and warned her to leave him alone. He reportedly told his mother, "This is my life. Leave me alone or I'll hurt you." Thus, he was left to his fate, more so when he was no longer a juvenile.

Ade's sojourn ended in the town some years later when news broke that he was arrested for armed robbery in another town. Everyone knew what happened to those arrested and convicted for armed robbery in the country. Back then, the crime carried the supreme penalty. Twenty children could not be together for twenty years, after all. The adults knew what they were talking about.

Ade's story sent a message to everyone in the town, and beyond. The youths understood that people could end up like Ade, but they did not see it happening so close to home. The reality dawned on everyone when it happened to someone they knew. Parents and guardians spoke with their wards about the cheerless incident. The event brought to memory one of the folktales told about the outcome of keeping bad companies.

Once upon a time, there was a child named Gbade. He was fortunate in every way one looked at life. His parents were prosperous ranch owners. They owned scores of goats, sheep, cattle, and horses at their stable. The family needed no introduction because it was famous and known far and wide.

Gbade could become the best he wanted. Many of his peers had little, but he had a lot of opportunities. Every boy wanted to be his friend, and the girls flocked to him. People thought Gbade would become the prosperous heir to his parents' estate in the future.

Regrettably, Gbade joined a group of never-do-well kids, who preferred to start life where they should end it. They had a preference for enjoyment when they should be working. The youth took joy in goofing around, as if life was trouble-free. They did not pay attention to anyone who tried to counsel them about life. It was jolly-go-round life every day.

"I cannot carry elephant meat on my head and dig the ground for cricket meat with my toes. I don't have to work so hard when my parents have everything ready for me," Gbade told everyone who requested him to work. While his peers worked so hard in the field, the boy would go to

The Hidden Treasures in Gray Hair

the palm-wine seller's booth with his friends. They would talk, laugh, and drink all day. In particular, they loved to talk about the good things of life, although they were not working to own them.

Gbade assumed that his friends cared so much about him. He did not realize they were milling around him because of who he was. He sometimes stole and slaughtered his parents' goats and sheep, and feasted with his associates. Gbade's parents were not aware of the frivolous celebrations. He reveled whenever his parents went out of town.

Eventually, words filtered to Gbade's parents that the young man wasn't doing anything other than reveling whenever his parents were out. Their son's way of life saddened them, and they determined to make him change. Gbade's parents loved him so dearly, but they knew they had to change his lackadaisical mind-set.

"Gbade, my son, hard work is the only remedy against poverty," advised his father. "Hard work makes people flourish and become famous. Those who recline when they should be preparing for the future suffer in the end."

"Do not rely on what we own right now," contributed Gbade's mother. "No one knows what tomorrow would bring. Life may play a trick on you if you wait on the livestock at the stable. Prosperity has no permanent friends; it stays with only those who treat it right." She said everything she could to get her son to change his slipshod way of life.

"We won't be here to provide for you forever," counseled Gbade's father. "Your mother and I own the ranch as a result of hard work. The livestock did not come to us out of the blue."

At first, Gbade thought about what his parents said. Somehow, he knew they were telling the truth. However, he listened to his friends' badly thought-out second opinions thereafter.

"You are just having some fun. You are not hurting anyone. It is those who lack fortune to fall back on who must work so hard. You don't have to sweat everyday when your parents have a large amount of livestock," Gbade's friends reassured him.

"So, my parents had been talking only so people won't think they were encouraging irresponsibility. Now, I get it." Gbade considered his friends' appalling advice and dumped his parents' profitable counseling.

Thereafter, it appeared like everything Gbade's parents said entered through his right ear and came out from the left, without his brain retaining anything. He did not argue with his parents, but he couldn't understand why they kept making a big deal out of his lifestyle. He believed that whatever his parents bequeathed him would be enough to continue with his laid-back existence.

The prodigal son did not change his lifestyle, after all. He pretended that he was working hard, but he did that to make his parents feel better.

The Hidden Treasures in Gray Hair

Gbade and his indolent friends stopped going to the palm-wine booth where people could see them. They made an arrangement with a palm-wine tapper to supply them at a hidden location.

Remember that Gbade's mother warned that life could play a trick on those who depended on handouts from parents without working hard. Her fear came to pass a couple of years later. There was a serious food shortage because rain did not fall and there was drought across the region. There was unexpected shortfall in crop harvest and livestock did not make it either.

Gbade's parents were no exception. They lost most of the livestock at their stable. The family could not afford as much food as they used to. The food sellers travelled many miles to buy food from other regions. Thus, their products were so expensive that many could not afford to buy as much as they needed.

Gbade's parents could not believe what happened to them during the depressive period. They became disheartened and grouchy after losing most of their livestock. They remained inconsolable for a long time, regardless of what people said to make them feel better. It was too much for them to bear the fact that fate treated the once affluent and famous family the way it did.

The family's fortune disappeared very rapidly. They had to sell the remaining livestock to buy the ever-expensive foodstuff. The friends of Gbade's parents could not help when they needed them most. The depression affected them, too. The once-extravagant Gbade could not believe his eyes when his friends, who could have helped, turned away from him. They argued that they must keep the little they had left, as no one knew when the depression would end. Gbade felt betrayed by his friends.

"Didn't I give these people food and money when I had it?" Gbade searched his soul. "I was there when they needed me. I never disappointed my friends, and they are now flaunting the reality of life in my face. Why didn't I listen to my parents? How come I assumed that life would ever remain jolly?"

There was no longer a free ride for Gbade and his once-ubiquitous friends. The young man's associates started dwindling till none of them showed up at his house again. Gbade felt miserable that his former friends flocked to him because of who he was. He felt sorry for himself and regretted his past life.

"I wish I had listened to my parents," Gbade thought as he regretted his newly found miserable life. "I wish I had taken life seriously, without allowing prosperity to pass me. I wish I had worked hard from sun-up to sun-down. I wish I had chosen my friends without allowing them to choose me because of who I was."

Things became so bad and Gbade couldn't feed himself. His parents had to let him go because he was now an adult. He went to his old friends, but they told him to leave. Gbade had nowhere to turn again, and he became a beggar. Unfortunately, most people had little to give during the famine. Most people were concerned about providing for their families than giving to others.

"My parents actually said nothing was written in stone in life," lamented Gbade. "They counseled me that the rich who became complacent could go broke, and the indigent who worked hard could strike it rich. I wish I had listened to them."

I would advise youths to choose their friends wisely. Those who goof around without taking life seriously will not inspire another person to be serious either. It is smart to choose hard-working and inspiring youths as friends, because they will inspire one to succeed. It is okay to have constructive fun, but associating with disruptive, disrespectful, and disgruntled youths is a recipe for failure.

Remember that the quality of the friendships you make says something about you. You could be levelheaded, but your friends' behaviors would rub off on you if they are not like you. Reasonable people shouldn't keep undisciplined associates anyway. People will judge you on the basis of whom you associate with. Good kids are sometimes categorized as bad ones when they associate with dire friends. You have nothing to lose when you ditch bad friends.

It is easy to fail when one hangs around happy-go-lucky people who see life as a joke. On the other hand, one feels challenged to achieve when he associates with rational and accountable people. I dared to achieve sometimes because of the quality of people I associated with. I realized it was easy to slack off when one associated with unchallenging people who did not take time seriously.

Chapter 5
TIME—The Consumable Entity

Time depletes like a piece of cake that disappears as one eats it. Every period spent wastefully is like a bad investment. It has the potential to haunt one in the later part of life.

A wooden clock was another status symbol of the late 1960s. It was one more yardstick for measuring how successful a family was. There were few of the elongated time-telling devices in town. Only the affluent households owned them. Most *wannabe* comfortable families had ordinary table clocks. The well-regarded wooden clocks came in two main sizes: standard and large.

Regardless of their sizes, the clocks had major things in common. They had wooden exteriors and glass faces. Many of them had brass dials with Roman numerals. Most had silvery pendulums that swung endlessly both sides. They all hung on the wall.

The more affluent people preferred the larger clocks that chimed or cooed like birds every hour. The clocks' radium-coated numerals, minute, and hour hands glowed softly in the dark. The kids whose families owned such clocks did not hesitate to talk about them when the opportunities presented themselves. That was an uncomplicated way to broadcast their families' class without stepping on other children's toes.

My aunt's family had two wooden clocks, and one of them chimed. Mama Oye, my mother's elder sister, was married to a cocoa store owner. A clock hung on the wall of each of their two lounges. I visited my aunt frequently, so I could listen to the chiming clock. The tolling mechanism fascinated me so much that I wished I could open the box to see what was inside.

"Listen to the clock with the pendulum. It chimes every hour—once at one o-clock, twice at two, thrice at three, and so on," said Olaolu, my cousin, as the clock's pendulum swung continuously. As usual, all of the kids in the lounge appeared curious, except the one who had recently returned from Lagos, the former federal capital city that every local boy aspired to visit someday.

"You haven't seen anything yet," said the boy from the city, as the other boys watched. "There are even bigger clocks with pendulums in Lagos. They are called the *grandfather clocks*. They are so large that people can't hang them on the wall.

The Hidden Treasures in Gray Hair

They stand on their own wooden feet, towering above people."

The Lagos owners of the grandfather clocks must be richer than our town's rich people, I thought, as I wished I could visit the city myself. The boy from the city talked a little more about the giant clocks, and ended by singing the grandfather clock's song, to the delight of the local kids:

> My grandfather's clock
> Was too large for the shelf,
> So it stood ninety years on the floor;
> It was taller by half
> Than the old man himself,
> Though it weighed not a penny weight more.
> It was bought on the morn
> Of the day he was born,
> And was always his treasure and pride;
> Ninety years without slumbering,
> Tick, tock, tick, tock,
> His life seconds numbering,
> Tick, tock, tick, tock,
> It stopped short
> Never to go again,
> When the old man died.

"We learned the song at school," the boy said proudly.

"They even sing exotic songs in Lagos schools," I hummed to myself. That made me hunger for the city more than ever.

Dele Ajaja

My grandfather had no wall clock. He did not even have a table clock or a wristwatch; instead he gauged time with the positions of the sun.

"It should be about four now. The sun has moved beyond *Omi Atan*; it is time to go home," said my grandfather as the sun went down the horizon beyond *Atan* pond, where we fetched water at one of his farms. Grandpa amazed me with the precise way he gauged time. He was rarely ten minutes over or less than the correct time.

Grandpa was mindful of time. He grabbed every chance he found to talk to me about the importance of time in life.

"Time flies. No one is smart enough to tie time down with a rope," said my grandfather while encouraging me to spend my time profitably. "Time waits for no one. It is short. It is not long as a street; it is not lengthy as the barrel of a gun. No one can afford to spend time extravagantly. The creator, who created time, even counts as it goes by."

By way of explaining why he often went to the farm early, Grandpa said, "It is the lazy man who sleeps till the sun licks the dew off the leaves along the path to the farm." Everyone knew he would be whistling the time-honored folk songs and removing the weeds at his farm by the time the sun came up.

The school took time seriously, too. Students were mandated to be punctual at every occasion. Everyone respected the "school bell" whenever it rang. The students would run and imitate the sound of the tire-rim metal as the time-keeper hit it with a short piece of metal:

> *Boys, girls, come to school*
> *Boys, girls, come to school*
> *Boys, girls, come to school*
> *Boys, girls, come to school...*

The teachers conveyed the idea that time was everything. Mr. Fasakin was a dedicated tutor—an unsurpassed educator who showed a lot of passion when it came to imparting wisdom to young people. He was a very compassionate man, but meant business when it came to punctuality. His students said he did not like it when someone came to his class late without a good alibi. He expected everyone to spend time judiciously.

Mr. Fasakin taught the senior classes. He did not teach the junior class to which I belonged then, but the senior teachers could address any class they wanted, if it was necessary. I saw Mr. Fasakin in action the day a girl from my class went to the teachers' lounge to report the boy who disturbed her.

Teachers usually allowed students to study on their own during the week before the examination. It was unusual for students to misbehave when they were by themselves. Those were the days when students kept the peace on their own, simply because the teachers said so earlier.

We expected an earful when Mr. Fasakin accompanied the girl back to the classroom. We all knew we should be studying for the approaching examination and not playing around. Most eyes gazed at the no-nonsense teacher, except a few that looked unpleasantly at the boy who got us into trouble.

"You should be preparing for your exam, and not playing wildly. Everything has its own time. There is a time to be born, and there is a time to die. There is a time to plant, and there is a time to harvest. There is a time to work, and there is a time to play," Mr. Fasakin explained, like a father addressing his children.

"Use every opportunity you have well, as it may never come your way again. Time doesn't come back after you waste it. You cannot eat your cake and have it, still." One could hear if a needle dropped as the teacher surveyed the room to make sure that everyone was paying attention. We all felt guilty as we knew he was telling the truth.

"By the way, who is married among you? Is there someone with children here?" the teacher asked. Everyone was surprised because we were obviously not old enough to marry, let alone have children. We realized that the teacher was going to tell us something unanticipated. We all fixed our eyes on Mr. Fasakin for an answer to the riddle.

"Nothing should distract you from getting education, now that you are young. You are not

The Hidden Treasures in Gray Hair

married, and you have no children yet. You cannot waste your time now and wait till you are old before attending school. You shouldn't wait till you have your own families. How many of you know adults who have children and also go to school at the same time?" All of the students shook their heads, but I raised mine.

"My father is about to complete his university education and my mother attends the college of education," I said, telling the class what most of them did not know about my family. A couple of my close friends knew, but the rest did not.

"It hasn't been easy. I've been living with my grandparents. My mother couldn't continue with her education immediately after I was born. She had to wait for me to grow up a little. Now, I wish I could spend some time with my parents, but they are in school." I knew I was providing the answer to the teacher's puzzle as he did not interrupt, and the students were interested in my story, too.

Mr. Fasakin nodded recurrently. I could tell that he understood and sympathized with me because of the hurtful circumstances that prevented me from seeing my parents as much as I wanted. I also knew that my response saved the class a lot of headaches, because the teacher relaxed and tried to make everyone feel comfortable. We all realized that the storm had passed and the teacher would be gentle with us.

"Ayodele has explained the whole thing," said Mr. Fasakin. "It is best to do things at the right time. Does someone still think that one should delay his or her education till he has a family?" The teacher's message was clear, but a particular student pushed for more explanations.

"Sir, does time really matter? I wouldn't worry about time, as long as people get education," the student remarked. He was trying to advocate that people should get education, no matter how late, but he did not place his point in perspective. Fortunately, the teacher did not hesitate to explain further.

"People shouldn't forsake education because they are old, but it is less burdensome when people are young and nothing distracts them," Mr. Fasakin explained calmly. "Who cares for your family if you are married and have children before you decide to go to school?"

"My parents or relatives would care for my family if I decide to go to school later in life," suggested the insatiable student.

"Your parents would not be around forever, and they don't have to carry your burden all of their lives. You could overload yourself if you leave what you should do today till tomorrow." Mr. Fasakin was patient as he clarified further.

The teacher's rationalization aligned with my circumstance, and I thought I should explain further to the other student how important it was to do things at the right time. I waited for Mr. Fasakin to complete his explanation before I explained

The Hidden Treasures in Gray Hair

that it was the one who felt something who knew it more than those who did not.

"Don't leave what you can do today till tomorrow," I counseled. "Tomorrow will come with its own burden. It would have been better if my parents had completed their education before having a child, and the family would have been able to spend more time together later."

I did not mind that my issue presented the opportunity to discuss the importance of time. I wanted the other students to understand that things would not get any better if they delayed them more than necessary. I did not want to hold on selfishly to my story when someone could learn from it.

"I appreciated the fact that my parents went to school later," I continued, "but I sometimes felt that my grandparents shouldn't bear the burden of raising me. The elderly people had to bear my yoke with theirs. That was because my parents did not complete their education before having a child."

"That's right." "That's true." "I agree with you." Those were some of the responses from the other members of the class. The student who started the debate agreed, too. He nodded his head repeatedly. Just then, another student added his own story to the discussion.

"It is best to get education when you have no extra baggage," began the third student. "My mother confessed that she gave up schooling after having a child. She was overwhelmed with caring for me, all by herself. My father wasn't able to help much because he didn't have a job."

I was glad that the impromptu debate ended amicably. Everyone learned something, and no one received punishment for disruptive behavior. We spent the rest of the period prudently, studying more diligently than ever. I reasoned that dire things sometimes happened so people could learn from them, and what happened in my class was certainly one of them.

"I won't wait till I have a beautiful wife and a buzzing baby before I get education," joked the boy whose action set off the debate. He apologized to the girl he'd offended. The girl no longer appeared offended after all. We all seemed satisfied with the good lessons we learned about life.

Time meant so much to society. The elders wanted the youth to spend their time equitably. People were critiqued based on what they did with their times. Understandably, society did everything including using folktales to make young people take time seriously. A particular folktale was told about *Ijapa*, the tricky tortoise who wasted time and faced the ceaseless consequence.

Once upon a time, long before *Ijapa* became bald, the animal had hair on his head. He sometimes groomed his hair and wore hats like the humans. The young Ijapa cared so much about his looks, so he dressed nicely and walked around

The Hidden Treasures in Gray Hair

town in style. He did not go to the farm with his parents and he avoided hard work that made people sweat because he despised getting dirty.

Ijapa maintained his squeaky-clean life in the town while his peers tended farms in the field. He lived on what his parents and relatives offered him, without thinking of the future. A couple of people advised the tortoise to work on the farm, because that was the only job available back then. However, Ijapa did not listen to them.

"Why do you bother me about the future, as if the world would end tomorrow morning?" he asked. "Can't you mind your own business and leave me alone. See, I'm still young, and I have a lot of time ahead of me. I could go to the field anytime I want and tend my own farm. Perhaps I'll start farming in a couple of years' time."

The tortoise did not take time seriously. He assumed that things would continue to favor him. He did not believe that everything had its own time. He actually thought that people could turn back time and make up for the lost periods. Ijapa continued to rely on his parents and relatives who supported his lazy lifestyle.

"Time is going, Ijapa. You cannot leave what you can do today till tomorrow," one of his neighbors advised. Ijapa walked away from the harmless fellow without listening to him. He even made unpleasant gestures at the neighbor, who did not do anything other than advise Ijapa to spend his time wisely.

"Everyone tries to tell me what to do as if my life is theirs," complained the tortoise. "Why can't people just face their own lives, instead of getting involved in other people's businesses? My parents are not complaining that they can no longer feed me, and I'm not begging neighbors for food either. I'm tired of people telling me what to do."

Everyone tried to advise Ijapa to no avail. Nobody was able to convince him that he was growing up and his parents would not be there forever to feed him. He did not understand that he may not be able to make up for the lost time. The tortoise continued with his stylish-without-substance lifestyle till he was old enough to marry.

The tricky animal developed a strong interest in marriage and he followed young women around. Some ladies flocked to him because he was very clean and he walked around town in style. Perhaps the ladies did not realize how lazy Ijapa was or they just did not care about his personal life. They thought he was one of the finest suitors they could find out there. Some of them would do anything to have Ijapa.

Ijapa finally settled for the young woman whose parents owned a large farm. The young groom's parents invited him and advised that they would support him one more time during his marriage ceremony. However, they warned that Ijapa should support himself and his family thereafter. The lazy animal agreed with his parents and began to plan for the nuptials.

The Hidden Treasures in Gray Hair

Everyone who knew Ijapa thought he would start farming now that he was planning to marry and raise a family. Unfortunately, the animal would not go to the farm. The new farming season slipped by without Ijapa selecting a plot of land. He fantasized with starting the largest farm and overtaking the best farmers in the land. However, those who knew Ijapa very well did not take him seriously.

"Stop underestimating me. My farm will be the largest in the whole region. Just give me some time, and I'll start farming," Ijapa told those who advised him to work. He loved greatness, but he lacked what it took to become a great animal. "Those of you who thought I couldn't plow the soil should watch out. My farm will put you to shame when I start during the new planting season."

Soon, Ijapa's marriage ceremony came and his parents were ready as they promised. They provided the goats, sheep, yams, bitter cola, cola nuts, and cowries needed for consummating the ceremonies. Ijapa's marriage ceremony looked normal because his parents and other members of his family supported him.

Ijapa's new bride went home with him that night and was welcomed by his family. Things appeared normal for a couple of weeks till Ijapa's parents invited him and advised that he should take his wife and start his own family elsewhere. His father and mother explained that they had supported him enough and he couldn't live on them forever.

The tortoise had no option other than to leave his parents and look for his own house. Some of Ijapa's friends promised to assist him one more time. They put a raffia house together, but they warned that they would not support Ijapa any further. Thus, he was on his own after the last round of support by his peers. Ijapa's friends had their own homes and farms.

Ijapa and his new wife moved to their new home and began living by themselves. He knew he would not be able to feed his wife and himself, so he started going to other people's ceremonies. He even went to the ceremonies to which he was not invited. Ijapa would eat so much at the parties and took some food home for his wife.

It was easy for Ijapa's wife to notice his parasitic lifestyle now that they were living by themselves. She did not like her husband's way of life, and she started resenting it.

"Why would you go to other people's celebrations uninvited and eat their food?" Ijapa's wife asked. "How long do you think we could thrive on other people's charity? I guessed I made a mistake by marrying a squeaky-clean, but indolent animal like you," Mrs. Ijapa lamented.

"Don't worry, Honey, I'll start farming shortly," Ijapa pleaded with his wife. He told her about his plan to look for a large portion of land and start the largest farm in the region. However, Ijapa's

The Hidden Treasures in Gray Hair

wife, whose parents were farmer, knew that the farming season was over, as people were about to start harvesting their crops.

"You can lie to someone else about farming, but you cannot lie to me," she responded. "I was born and raised on a farm. I know when and what people put into farming. Serious farmers don't go to other people's celebrations uninvited to eat and bring home food for the other members of their families."

Soon, there was no food in Ijapa's house, and things became tough for the couple. Ijapa finally went to the field to tend a farm. Unfortunately, he had nothing to do, because it was harvesting season. He had nothing to harvest because he did not sow anything. Remember that everything had its own time—time to sow and time to reap.

The couple sat and looked at each other for a while. Ijapa's wife was not happy, but she suggested that they should visit her parents and eat over there. Ijapa did not like the suggestion, but he had no better option. He did not want his wife's family to know that he could not provide for her.

"Okay, we can visit your parents, but I won't eat there," said Ijapa. He was terribly ashamed of himself. He regretted the years he'd wasted by going around town and doing nothing in particular. He realized that he could not care for a family like his peers. Ijapa wished he could roll back his life and make up for the lost time, but it was too late.

"No one can turn back time," admonished Mrs. Ijapa. "Those who waste time by doing nothing end up regretting when their peers relish the fruits of their hard work. You went round the town pretending to be who you were not, and now everyone could see how naked you are. You could deceive people occasionally, but you cannot deceive them throughout your lifetime."

The couple arrived at the woman's parents' house later, and Ijapa's in-laws welcomed them nicely. The tortoise's in-laws were not aware that the animal was so lazy and could not provide for his family. It was harvesting season and Ijapa's in-laws had a lot of food in their storage. They cooked a delicious pot of beans.

The hungry animal could not stop savoring the food's aroma as his wife's mother cooked. He sniffed and sniffed, and wished he could sneak into the kitchen and have a mouthful of the delicious food. Soon, Ijapa stood up and started pacing around the living room. His wife did not know why her husband was moving around the place, so she started asking questions.

"Why are you pacing all over the place? Is something wrong with you, Ijapa? Could it be that you are so hungry and can't control yourself?" The woman became upset with her husband's behavior. She hoped that the animal would not disgrace himself at her parents' place.

"Hungry? Who says I'm hungry? I'm thinking of how large my farm will be when I start, and how

The Hidden Treasures in Gray Hair

I will work and walk all over the place," Ijapa lied to his wife. He couldn't humble himself and have a grip on reality. He continued to fantasize about owning the largest farm in the region even when he failed to act like a real farmer.

Soon, Ijapa's in-law finished cooking the meal and invited everyone to the table. Everyone else went to the table to eat, except Ijapa, who insisted that he was not hungry. Of course, he was very hungry, but he was too ashamed to admit that he came to his in-laws' house because of hunger. His wife knew he was hungry, but she did not want to expose Ijapa. She knew her parents would be disappointed that she'd married a lazy animal.

"I'm fine. I don't eat in the morning. I'm too busy at the farm in the morning and I eat only in the afternoon, after a hard day's work," Ijapa lied again. His wife stared at him maliciously, but she was careful so her parents would not notice. She was embarrassed that she'd ended up with the lazy and lying tortoise.

All ate until they were full, but the pot of beans was nowhere empty. They barely ate half of its contents. There was enough left for more people. Ijapa became impatient as he swallowed hard. He prayed that the people should move away from the kitchen, so he could have a bite of the delicious meal.

Ijapa's wish came to pass shortly as people moved away from the kitchen to the other parts of the building. The lazy animal snuck into the kitchen and opened the pot of beans. Ijapa took bite after bite of the food without getting caught. He couldn't stop eating because the food was truly delicious.

    The tortoise felt better after stealing some food. He played with his in-laws till late afternoon. Thereafter, it was time for him and his wife to depart. Ijapa's mother-in-law requested him to eat before they departed, as the tortoise said he usually ate late in the afternoon. Still, Ijapa would not swallow his pride and eat.

    "I'm fine. I don't have to eat now. I sometimes wait till late in the evening before I eat," Ijapa lied to his in-laws again. However, he was praying for one more chance to enter the kitchen and eat some of the beans before returning home with his wife. He could not afford to leave his in-laws without taking another bite because he had nothing to fall on at home.

    Ijapa was lucky once again as nobody noticed as he snuck back into the kitchen. The pot of beans was still hot because it remained on the sizzling earthen stove. He took a spoonful of the yummy food and tried to down it into his throat. Suddenly, something unpleasant happened. Ijapa heard footsteps as someone approached the kitchen.

    The tortoise quickly removed his hat and poured the scorching beans on his head. Then, he covered his head with the hat once again. He stepped out of the kitchen and joined the other

The Hidden Treasures in Gray Hair

members of the family in the living room. Nobody noticed what Ijapa had done immediately. Everything appeared normal as he threw banters at everyone.

"We must leave now!" Ijapa said suddenly as the searing food scorched his head. He swallowed hard as he sweated profusely. He paced all over the living room more than ever, and everyone was surprised at his bizarre conduct. Not even Ijapa's wife understood her husband's unusual behavior.

"It is against the tradition for someone to hurry away from his in-laws' house without a good reason," said Ijapa's father-in-law. He appealed to the animal to be patient and let them complete the usual departure observance. He held Ijapa's hands in an attempt to say goodbye, but the tortoise withdrew his hands. The ridiculous tortoise removed his hat, as he could no longer bear the pains.

Everyone found out the reason behind Ijapa's weird behavior as he brushed the hot food off his head. The tortoise's wife and the other members of her family were very upset and disappointed in Ijapa. They emptied their minds while expressing disappointments in no uncertain terms.

Ijapa's wife was particularly ashamed that her husband behaved that way at her parents' house. She could not look at his head the second time as Ijapa's hair was gone. The sweltering beans had scorched his head bare. Ijapa's in-laws were thoroughly embarrassed by their son-in-law's shameful action. They gasped for air as they struggled with emotion. They could not understand why Ijapa had snuck into the kitchen to steal hot beans when he could have eaten as much as he wanted without anyone raising an eyebrow.

"I apologize," the tortoise begged with shame. "I'm so ashamed of myself. I had all of the time to work hard, like everyone else, but I did nothing. I cannot turn back time after I squandered it all. Now, I have to suffer the consequences. I surely deserve whatever I get now." That was the reason behind tortoise's baldness till today. The outlandish animal was very sad and angry with himself.

Chapter 6
ANGER—The Sightless Zone

Anger comes naturally when circumstance permits it. But don't allow it to blind you. He whom anger blinds takes a flight from the precinct of reason and lands at the sightless zone of insanity.

Dayo became my friend by chance. Those who befriended one another in the town belonged to the same age bracket. Friends were rarely more than two years younger or older than one another, but I was about five years older than Dayo. We did not visit each other regularly as standard friends did, but we recognized one another as friends whenever and wherever we met.

It was the kind of friendship ordained by providence. We would not have become friends if we had based our association on age, according to that region's custom. However, we became friends through a common process. I did Dayo a favor and he appreciated my gesture. I acted like his big brother when he needed one.

Dayo was a healthy child. He cherished the hustle and bustle of activities engaged by the kids around him, and wanted to be a part of them. He tried all he could to fit in with the other children. He was a friendly and harmless child, loved and admired by most children. However, a few made fun of him because of the challenge he faced. Dayo couldn't talk, and he was also hard of hearing.

Dayo noticed the things around him like other children, and he had feelings like his peers. He was very polite and he possessed the positive attributes of a good child. His smartness reflected in his ability to transcend his challenges. He understood what others said by reading their lips, and he communicated satisfactorily with hand and body gestures. To me, he was a normal child.

I met Dayo for the first time when two kids made fun of him in my neighborhood. I did not expect anyone to laugh at someone who had a disability that wasn't his own fault. However, the two immature kids proved me wrong by doing just that. That was one of the times I learned that human behaviors may not be fully predictable after all.

"*Beh-jeh-jeh-hee!*" shouted one of the two kids.

The other boy started laughing viciously and repeating the slandering utterance, "*beh-jeh-jeh-hee!*"

The Hidden Treasures in Gray Hair

That was the usual sound Dayo uttered, in addition to hand and body gestures, whenever he communicated with people. I never saw anything funny in the way Dayo communicated, and I did not expect anyone to laugh at him either.

"Be quiet! The two of you should be ashamed of yourselves for being bullies," I said in disgust. I was upset by the reckless kids' actions and reprimanded them immediately.

"I will report you to your parents if you don't apologize to this boy right now. You should have known that it wasn't his choice to communicate that way." I insisted that the offending kids should make an apology for their shameful behaviors.

Good enough, they apologized to Dayo and even shook hands with him. The bullied boy understood what I had done and appreciated the outcome of my action. He showed gratitude in turn by shaking hands with me. Everyone dispersed from the spot and went home without further hitches.

I was not surprised when Dayo visited me a couple of days later. He made the usual sound and gestures as he explained how I'd protected him from the boys who bullied him a few days earlier. My grandmother was very pleased with what I did. She welcomed Dayo pleasantly and cooked for the two of us.

We were not related, but Dayo started looking up to me as his big brother, and I graciously accepted the new role. No one dared bully him in my presence. Some couldn't even do it in my absence, because they thought I would find out. Most children treated Dayo with respect at the playground and along the street whenever I was around.

Unfortunately, I wasn't around Dayo all of the time. Although most children liked and treated him nicely, a few disrespectful kids did not stop making fun of him whenever there was nobody to stop them. The careless kids sometimes pestered Dayo with insulting jokes.

Dayo became angry one evening and chased two erring kids around with a piece of wood. He did not stop till the boys ran across a couple of streets from the playground. Apparently, a lot of people witnessed that incident. I learned about it the following day when one of the kids' mothers described Dayo as "a troublesome kid."

"That boy chased my son and his friend with a stick all over the town," she stated, while painting a bad picture of Dayo.

"Your son and his friend were not innocent as you thought," I advised the woman. "A handful of kids, including your son and his friend, harass Dayo occasionally. Why would anyone bother someone with a disability that wasn't his fault?"

Regrettably, the bothersome boy's mother blamed Dayo for overreacting to a little teasing by fellow teenagers. She transferred that impression to whoever listened to her story. Although the majority of the people understood that Dayo

The Hidden Treasures in Gray Hair

did not start the problem, some agreed with the woman's tale.

Some of those who agreed with the woman only heard half of the story. They did not witness or hear the other half that showed Dayo as the original victim of the little neighborhood bullies. They had no clue about the mental agony the bullied boy went through before caving under the pressure of anger.

Clearly, Dayo did not start the problem. The insensitive kids who made fun of him did. Those who understood the whole story did not expect people to blame Dayo for the whole incident. They thought the boy was forced to stand up for himself. However, I figured out where Dayo went wrong in the whole dispute. People could learn something from my little friend's story.

Anger is a natural phenomenon. People have reasons to be angry occasionally. Anger comes when the circumstances are right for it. Being angry may not be a problem, but what people do with their anger could become a problem after all.

Dayo had a good reason to be angry, but he ended up being perceived as the problem because of how he handled his anger. Could he have done something differently? Certainly, he could have reported the pushy boys to their parents or other adults who cared. Then someone could have intervened on his behalf.

As usual, I would have talked to the erring boys if Dayo had reported them to me. He could have also reported the incident to his own parents. Unfortunately, he thought he could take care of the problem on his own. Children can take care of some problems by themselves, but it is better to allow adults to solve certain problems for them.

Those who thought Dayo was the problem did not know why he became so angry, but they saw him chasing his tormentors with a stick. They witnessed Dayo as the aggressor, but did not witness him as the victim of a protracted bullying saga.

Sometimes, the way one reacts to an initial maltreatment determines whether passersby would support or go against the victim. Responding violently to the issue could turn the victim to the aggressor. For instance, people may not hear someone calling you names, but they might see you punching the person in response. Then you could end up becoming the attacker instead of the attacked.

Violence is not a good response to an act of injustice. Most of the time, violence does nothing than breeding further violence. It turns people against the wronged party and the scoundrel appears like the casualty. Violence simply turns the victim to the villain, and the latter ends up as the afterthought victim.

I communicated with Dayo, my younger friend, thereafter. I explained that the appropriate response to an act of aggression was to allow

The Hidden Treasures in Gray Hair

people to see or know what an aggressor did to him. I clarified that he should have asked an adult to help him. Otherwise, those who did not know what the aggressors did, but saw him responding aggressively, would see him as the problem.

Anger was never a winner. The elders counseled against it and schools taught students to avoid it. They told the stories of the victims who engaged peace, instead of violence, in response to the harm done to them. The historical victims won the fights of their lives without engaging in violence.

It is unsafe to respond violently to an act of injustice. The aggressive individual who started the problem could end up engaging in more violence against the victim. Thereafter, the victim could end up as a perpetual victim. Perhaps nothing is more painful than remaining the victim always. My history teacher talked about this in the classroom.

"Mahatma Gandhi and his fellow Indians had a good reason to be angry. But Gandhi, the great leader, counseled his followers against violence," Ms. Ogunrinde explained to us in history class. She told the story of how the leader steered his people away from violence against the British.

"Gandhi advocated peaceful protests instead of a violent response against the British Empire. The Indians gained independence without making violence the centerpiece of their fight.

"The African Americans couldn't have defeated the white majority if the former had engaged violence. However, Martin Luther King Junior advocated a nonviolent fight against the white majority of that time, and the black people gained their freedom."

I listened with rapt attention, as did everyone else in the classroom. Nothing enthralled students more than when a good teacher told the story that fascinated them. Everyone liked the story of the oppressed that triumphed after his travails. We wanted more of that story, and the teacher did not disappoint us.

"Kwame Nkrumah of Ghana and many other African liberationists were peaceful while seeking independence from the colonialists. Many of those who sought self-determination won sovereignty for their countries without shooting a single bullet."

The story of the legendary Madiba Rolihlahla Nelson Mandela of South Africa fascinated the students more than ever. His was a classic example of what peaceful approach could achieve, compared to the animosities and damages that violence could do to noble causes.

"Nelson Mandela could have received the death penalty if he had engaged in violence, but he ended up as a hero worldwide because of his peaceful approach," explained Ms. Ogunrinde. What the teacher said made a lot of sense to me and the other students.

The Hidden Treasures in Gray Hair

Many expected Mandela to give up his diplomatic approach after he was sentenced to the notorious apartheid prison at Robin Island. However, the famous prisoner number 46664 remained fascinated with non-violence. Mandela taught the world a great lesson by embracing non-violence during his twenty-seven-year sojourn at the maximum-security prison intended for hardened criminals.

Nelson Mandela forgave his detractors and later became the first African president of South Africa. The wide-reaching leader advocated forgiveness and unanimity among the diverse races and cultures in his country. Mandela did not stray away from his non-violence message years after he gave up South African presidency. He continued with his message of love to fellow South Africans and the world at his Transkei hometown of Qunu.

Ms. Ogunrinde would not stop talking about lessons in non-violence till she mentioned Desmond Tutu, a Nobel Peace Prize–winning religious leader, who also embraced non-violence as the appropriate solution to the apartheid problem in South Africa. The outstanding leader chose peace over resolving issues with guns and ammunitions.

Many folktales were told about how anger could damage good causes and turn the victims to the villains. Perhaps the most popular one in that region was how the pig hurt his own cause by resulting to violence. Ijapa, the villainous animal in the story, took advantage of the pig's anger.

Once upon a time, the pig and the tortoise were friends. Everyone in the town knew them as pals. They did a lot of things together, and they often support one another. Thus, it was not unusual when the tortoise asked the pig to lend him some money.

"Pig, my friend, you are the best friend anyone could have," began the crafty tortoise. "You helped me when I needed help, and you supported me when I needed support. I need your assistance once again. Would you loan me some money for a couple of weeks?"

"Money cannot stand between friends. I have the moral obligation to loan you money if I can. That's what friends are for. I will loan you money if I have the amount you are looking for," the pig explained. He thought that was a good way to demonstrate his affability to his friend.

"Thank you, my friend. I knew I could depend on you," the tortoise praised. He knew that the pig would loan him the money anyway. After all, that was not the first time the pig had done him a favor.

"By the way, how much do you need?" the pig asked his friend.

"I need fifty cowries. I have to place a stronger roof on my house before the raining season begins."

The Hidden Treasures in Gray Hair

"Expect me at dawn tomorrow. I'll bring the money to you myself," said the kind-hearted pig. As usual, he kept his promise by knocking at the tortoise's door first thing in the morning. He handed his friend the money as he promised.

"Thank you for being there for me every time I need help," said the tortoise. "Trust me, I promise to repay you in five weeks."

The pig departed happily with the feeling that he had done the right thing. After all, they say, a friend in need is a friend indeed. On the other hand, the tortoise appeared like a conqueror. He did not have the intention to repay his friend. He had a sinister plan to avoid repaying the pig.

The five weeks promised by Ijapa passed, but the pig did not suspect anything unusual. He did not ask for the money immediately, because he thought his friend needed a few weeks more. Ijapa, too, did not talk about the money. He continued his life as usual, as if he did not owe the pig.

Five additional weeks passed, and Ijapa did not say anything about the money. The pig thought it was time for him to say something, if the friend he did a favor for failed to repay or say something about the money. He went to Ijapa's house one afternoon to confront him about the latter's lack of courtesy.

"You surprised me, Ijapa my friend," started the pig. "Courtesy demands that you keep your promise when you borrow money from someone. You borrowed money for five weeks, but ten weeks have passed without you paying. Besides, you have not said anything about the money."

"I'm sorry, my friend. Please, give me five more weeks. I'm going through a hard time right now. I'll surely pay you then." The tortoise pleaded that the pig should give him further moratorium. Yet, he knew he would not repay the money in five weeks' time.

"Fine! I will give you five more weeks to pay," the pig said as he departed. He had no idea that his friend did not plan to pay him the money.

As before, another five weeks passed without Ijapa mentioning the money or saying something about it. The pig was upset by his friend's lack of courtesy. He went to Ijapa's house again to ask for his money. However, the crafty tortoise was into another of his many antics.

Ijapa spotted the pig as he approached his house. The tortoise quickly rubbed oil and sprinkled water on his face. Then he ran to his bed and covered himself with a blanket. He instructed his wife, *Yannibo*, to tell the pig that he had been sick for a while.

"You must pay my money today," the pig said as he entered Ijapa's house.

"Pig, I'm sure you were not aware," Yannibo said. "I'm sorry but your friend has been sick for a while. That's why he has not paid the money he owed you. Please, give him another five weeks."

"I'm sorry that Ijapa has been sick," the pig said as he watched his friend groaning in bed. "I'll

The Hidden Treasures in Gray Hair

surely give him another five weeks. Please, Yannibo let me know if there is something I could do to help." The pig hung around a while to sympathize with his friend before departing.

The new moratorium of five weeks passed, but the pig did not ask Ijapa the money. He thought he should give his friend more time to heal before bothering him. Thus, he only went to visit Ijapa to find out how he was doing. The pig was happy that Ijapa looked healthy when he visited him. The former entered Ijapa's house unannounced that day.

The pig went to Ijapa's house again after a few weeks. He tried to be gentle with Ijapa, because he thought his friend just emerged from a serious illness. Unfortunately, Ijapa asked for more time.

"I'm sorry that I've not been able to pay you," pleaded the tortoise. "I will surely pay you in five weeks' time, if you could give me that much time." He said as he made up excuses for not honoring his promises.

It occurred to the pig at that time that Ijapa was not going to pay the money he owed him. He realized that Ijapa had not made any efforts or said anything about the money till he, the pig, asked for it.

"You did not honor any of your promises! I'll give you the usual five weeks you asked for. Unfailingly, I'll get my money from you in five weeks' time." The pig said and stormed out of Ijapa's house.

Obviously, the pig had enough reasons to be angry, and he was really angry at the tortoise. He planned that he would leave no stone unturned to get his money back the next time he visited Ijapa. Thus, he allowed the extra five weeks requested by Ijapa to pass before trying again.

The pig was ready on the day Ijapa promised to pay him. He trekked to the latter's house as quick as he could. The debtor expected his friend to come for his money that day, so he was ready to play another trick on him. Ijapa sported the pig as he approached his house.

The tricky tortoise had made an arrangement with his wife, Yannibo. He requested her to overturn him as soon as the pig approached the house, so his back could be on the ground and his chest facing upward. Yannibo did as her husband told her. She overturned Ijapa, and he looked like a grinding stone as he rested on his back.

Yannibo quickly placed a handful of pepper on her husband's chest and started grinding it with a small stone. The pig stormed into the house shortly. Ijapa knew that the pig would be very angry, and he planned to take advantage of his anger.

Ijapa had instructed his wife to grind the pepper on his chest, without answering the pig's questions when he entered. He expected his generous friend to do something unexpected when blinded

The Hidden Treasures in Gray Hair

by anger. The pig saw Ijapa's wife grinding pepper as he entered the house.

"Where is Ijapa?" the tempestuous pig asked Yannibo, who pretended to be busy grinding pepper. She did not answer the pig, as instructed by her husband. The pig became angrier at that point.

"Didn't you hear me, Yannibo? Tell me, where is your husband? I must collect my money today," the pig said as he shuddered with anger.

"Can't you see that I'm busy, Mr. Pig?" Yannibo said and continued to grind the pepper on her husband's chest.

"You dare not insult me after your husband failed to pay what he owed me," the pig said. He bended down and grabbed what he perceived as the grinding stone. He did not realize that the "stone" was his ungrateful friend, Ijapa. The pig went outside the house and threw the grinding stone to the bush.

"Now, answer me, Yannibo. Where is your husband? I must collect my fifty cowries today." The pig said. The angry animal ransacked the house, thinking that Ijapa was hiding from him. The pig did not give up looking for Ijapa as he looked everywhere.

Ijapa, who landed on the lush weeds in the bush, was not hurt. He stood up immediately and started running toward his house. He was happy that the pig did exactly as he expected. Now, he would make his friend pay for allowing anger to overwhelm him.

"How are you, Pig, my friend?" Ijapa said as he ran into the house, panting. "I went somewhere very important, but ran back home, so I could pay you your money. I knew you have been patient with me over the weeks."

"Not so fast, Ijapa, my husband." Yannibo said. "The pig wants you to pay what you owed him, but he has to pay for the grinding stone he threw away."

"What grinding stone are you talking about, Yannibo? Certainly, you are not talking about the expensive stone I bought for one hundred cowries." Ijapa said, pretending not to believe what his wife was saying.

"Of course, I'm talking about the expensive stone you bought to commemorate our wedding anniversary," retorted Yannibo as she played along with her husband's trick. They were determined to use the pig's anger against him.

"Pig, my friend, I owed you only fifty cowries, but you threw away the grinding stone that cost one hundred cowries. You must pay me the one hundred cowries, if you want your fifty cowries back." Ijapa said.

The tortoise invited his neighbors and everyone who cared to listen to his story. He told them his version of the story. Unfortunately, the trapped pig had nothing to say to defend himself. Every-

The Hidden Treasures in Gray Hair

one blamed the pig for overreacting and throwing away Ijapa's stone.

"I'm so sorry, Ijapa, my friend. I'll look for the grinding stone. I didn't throw it far away from here." The poor pig went to the nearby bush and started scooping the ground with his snout, looking for Ijapa's grinding stone. That's why pigs scoop the ground with their snouts till today.

The pig ended as the villain, instead of the innocent victim he was. He allowed anger to blind him and he found himself in the sightless zone. The tricky tortoise was full of pride as he derided his former friend.

Chapter 7
PRIDE—The Pretty and the Monster

What you intend as music could sound like noise if it is not well arranged. It is good to take pride in what you have, but it becomes unpleasant when you flaunt it inordinately.

Uncle Soji was my idol. He made me proud. He was the first to bring high-level academic honor to the extended family. I was young when he went to England for further studies, but I remember when he returned home with academic accomplishments. He was one of the rare holders of the Doctor of Philosophy degree in the district. Everyone was ecstatic about the hero's homecoming.

"My uncle would return from the white man's land next month," I told my classmates at school. I also informed my associates in the neighborhood. I started the countdown soon after I overheard Grandma telling her friends at the women's association she belonged to. My grandmother was *Baba Ofi's* (Uncle Soji's father) older sister.

Uncle Soji's return was a source of pride for all. It was something to cheer about. Positive pride is about having a sense of worth and being pleased with what you have. It is good to have pride in one's personal accomplishments. One could have pride in his family's achievements. It is all right to have pride in one's country and the nation's symbols of sovereignty.

"The people of London should have pride in the newly constructed London Bridge," said Mr. Fakayode, my elementary school teacher. He was talking about the bridge over the River Thames in social studies class. The knowledgeable teacher described the bridge as a suitable structure that should make the people of London proud.

I was blessed with some of the greatest teachers ever. They talked about many things the diverse peoples of the world were proud of. The Egyptians were proud of the Sphinx and the pyramids of Giza, near Cairo. The great structures, erected centuries ago near the great Nile River, were commissioned by the pharaohs, the late kings of Egypt. The Egyptians continue to have pride in those monuments as you read this.

In modern times, the people of the United States of America have pride in the Statue of Liberty—the famous monument on Liberty Island in the scenic New York Harbor. The people of France presented the statue to the people of the United

The Hidden Treasures in Gray Hair

States to mark the 1886 centennial of the declaration of independence by the original colonies (states) of the United States.

The French people have something to be proud of, too—the Eiffel Tower. The giant metal structure that stands head and shoulders above the city of Paris is known around the world as the symbol of France. People say whoever visits Paris without seeing the Eiffel Tower by the Seine River has not visited France.

What are the people of Greece proud of? The Parthenon remains Greece's best-known monument around the world. The renowned cultural edifice was reportedly built for Athena, the ancient Greek goddess, in the fifth century BC. The Parthenon is the pride of Greece as the eyes are the pride of the face.

The Taj Mahal is one of India's foremost cultural monuments. It was purportedly built by Shah Jaha, an Indian emperor, in remembrance of his desired wife, Mumtaz Mahal, some centuries ago. The mausoleum is known worldwide as one of its kind. Indians have a reason to be proud of the Taj Mahal and their other monuments.

The Great Wall of China, claimed by some to be visible from the space, made the old China great. It remains a thrilling glory today as it makes modern China great. China has made giant strides in economic, industrial, and military accomplishments, but the Great Wall remains a major national showcase.

Did you know that the Panama Canal, a manmade water channel, connects the Pacific and the Atlantic oceans? Panamanians are proud that their nation makes shipping easier, quicker, and more profitable. Ships from the Atlantic do not have to travel all the way down to the tip of South America before reaching the Pacific side of the Americas.

The Australians celebrate the Sydney Harbor Bridge, the arch bridge made of steel. The "Coathanger," as it's known by Sydney residents, connects the northern and the southern ends of the Sydney harbor. It was constructed many years ago.

Still talking about pride, it is okay to be proud of one's former and current schools, and the good things they stand for. One could even take pride in his hometown and its accomplishments over the years. As a matter of fact, youths were taught to be proud of their native towns in the region where I grew up. These were positive aspects of pride that people talked about without losing face, as long as they did not go to the extreme.

We have learned about the pretty side of pride. The ugly side of pride looks like a monster that nobody wants. It is neither good for its perpetrator nor the bystanders. The ugly side of pride, they say, comes before fall. Whoever wants to ridicule himself should acquire the inordinate type of pride.

The Hidden Treasures in Gray Hair

The adults said one should limit his or her speeches or actions to the positive side of pride when talking about personal or family accomplishments. For instance, it was offensive for the king's son to go around town misbehaving and justifying his actions by saying, "I'm the prince, after all."

"Cover your mouth while eating if you have a good harvest during a famine," went an old saying. They said it was not a good idea to flaunt a sumptuous harvest during a food shortage, especially when you did not intend to share with others. This means, be careful how you brag about your special endowment or talent when others lack such an opportunity.

This extends to how you behave if you have something special or know how to do something better than the others. An accomplished sportsman or a celebrity is expected to watch his or her actions and speeches in a public place. He or she is expected to behave as a good role model.

It is okay to share one's accomplishments with others. There is a difference between responsible sharing and unwarranted bragging about something. You could encourage others, especially the youth, to learn from your success, when you talk about your achievement responsibly. However, it is different when you tell others that you are better than them because you are more talented.

Your accomplishment, class or status places you in a "fishbowl" where everyone watches every move you make. People are interested in what you have to say every time you open your mouth. They even want to know what you are chewing if your mouth moves. Whatever you do means something, compared to what an ordinary person does.

People may not take note of some things you do or say when you are an ordinary person. However, things change as soon as your status changes for the better. Some people would even hold on to some things you say when you mean no harm to anyone. Every word that comes out of your mouth is subject to some interpretations.

Someone looks up to every celebrity or a successful person. Many look up to you as you move up the social ladder in life. They watch everything you do; listen to every word you say; and take note of every unspoken gesture you make. Many expect role models to be perfect. There are no perfect beings anywhere; but those who want people to be proud of them aspire to be good. You could become one of them if you try.

A lot of talented youth allow pride to trap them. They cannot manage their endowments with good character. Their talents tried to push them up the social ladder, but pride brings them the other way. I knew some talented youths who would have been successful, but ended up going downhill because pride did not allow them to manage their successes well.

The Hidden Treasures in Gray Hair

Falah was a good soccer player. He could dribble more than many of his team members. Additionally, he had the stamina to run and hold the ball more than the others. There was hardly a match without Falah scoring a goal or two. Unfortunately, he had something else going. Falah's talent got into his head more than it should.

Everyone expected Falah to be the captain of his team, but the sports teacher refused. Those who witnessed the young man playing without knowing him very well expected him to be rewarded with being the team leader. Nevertheless, those who knew Falah very well knew the reason why he should not be the head.

"Falah is disrespectful to me and the members of the team," said the sports teacher. "Knowing he is the best player in the team, he comes to practice late; he dresses any way he wants; and talks to everyone anyhow. No team thrives without discipline—especially when the captain is not disciplined."

The young and dramatic soccer player who could have moved up rapidly ended up losing it all because his star dimmed gradually, till he stopped playing soccer altogether. He did not do well academically after all.

What about the snobbish girl who featured in a soap opera? She had all it took to be successful—she was pretty, she played her role very well, and she was admired by her fans. Those who favored her believed she had a future in acting and would remain on TV for many years to come.

Unfortunately, pride did not allow the attractive girl to go far. First, she thought she was better than her peers. She stopped associating with her old friends and started going about with the other pompous celebrities. Then, she started associating with those who were far older than her.

The soap opera ended after a couple of years. However, no new show accepted the girl. Those who knew her thought pride had made her lose touch with reality. A tabloid said the erstwhile trendy TV girl lost it all when she started associating with people of shady character. She was allegedly introduced to illegal drugs, and other illicit things crawled into her life.

LB was another talented youth who allowed pride to derail his career. He was a talented singer. He released a popular album very early in his career. The well-liked album launched him to instant success. Unfortunately, that got into LB's head, and he flaunted his achievement inordinately. Then his fame spiraled down as fast as it came. That marked the beginning and the end of LB's fame.

What happened to the above individuals could happen to the brilliant youths who spend more time disrespecting their teachers and classmates than studying. Many bright students who should be making the best grades are making lower ones because of undue pride. They pay more attention to their physical gifts than their responsibilities.

Ill pride wrecks people as wrecking balls wreck walls. It makes someone look obnoxious to others, and it sets the world against its perpetrator. Negative pride distorts the real person in its doer, and sends the wrong message about the person. It is easy for the world to see the dirty side of a boastful person.

Many folktales were told about ill pride. The stories warned about the danger of allowing pride to ruin one's life and career. They illustrated how pride could become a clog in the wheel of an erstwhile positively-viewed person. One of such stories was about the tricky tortoise and a boastful elephant.

Once upon a time, there was a boastful elephant. He was full of pride while dealing with the other animals. He looked down on others because he was bigger than them. The elephant took advantage of his huge size and demeaned others every time.

All animals understood that the elephant was the largest beast in the animal kingdom, and they respected him for that. However, he asked for more than he deserved. He wanted the other animals to worship him. The elephant reminded everyone about his size and muscle, even when it was not necessary.

"I'm the largest creature in the animal kingdom," he boasted. "All animals should bow down to me. Else, I would squash whoever refuses to do so."

The other animals had no choice than abide by the gigantic beast's uncivilized demands. The elephant dealt ruthlessly with some of the animals that dared him. He thrashed the lion, tiger, jaguar, cheetah, leopard, lynx, and caracal who challenged his authority.

All animals were forced to take orders from the harsh elephant. Many went to his house to bow down to him every morning. They brought food and gifts to the self-imposed king of the savanna. They sang his adoration even when they did not like him with all of their hearts.

"All animals are subject to my orders and requests. All must bring gifts to me. Whoever dares me is on the wrong side of my favor. I cannot guarantee the safety of the animals that disobey my requests. The king has spoken," the elephant said with a tone of finality.

Some of the powerful animals met and attempted to stop the harassment. However, the elephant broke up their meetings. He swatted some with his trunk and impaled the others with his tusks. The powerful animals went in different directions and never met to talk about the elephant again.

"No animal should meet and discuss how I run the animal kingdom," the dictatorial elephant decreed. "Whoever talks about me shall be put to death. I cannot watch you engage in mutinous activities against the constituted government of the animal kingdom ever again."

The elephant forgot that he had imposed himself on the animals, and nobody had made him the king of the animal kingdom. He spoke as if he was elected by the animals to run their affairs. He continued to misappropriate the animals' mandate. The elephant even forced some of the animals who rebelled against him into exile.

The demeaning was not limited to the animals alone. The elephant dared the humans, too. He went on rampage and destroyed their farms and huts occasionally. The giant animal killed a couple of the humans who tried to track him down. There were food shortages among the humans because the elephant destroyed their farms and poached their barns.

The animals were not the only ones desperate to get even with the elephant. The humans were equally mad at him. They wanted to get rid of the elephant so badly that they were willing to do anything. The humans did not understand why the elephant extended the lawlessness he created in the animal kingdom to their domain.

The humans accepted some of the animals who sought refuge from mankind—including the cow, dog, cat, horse, goat, sheep, and a few others. The humans were looking for a way to hold the elephant accountable for his out-of-touch behaviors.

"We welcome you to our domain," said the village chief to the animals that were seeking refuge. "You are all living witnesses of the elephant's uncultured manners. It is time for us, humans and animals, to work together and get him out of the way. How do we do that?"

The animals looked at one another and remained silent, just like the humans. No one was ready to risk death by haunting the rampaging elephant. After all, he had killed a couple of humans and many animals. Everyone preferred to stay beyond an arm's length from the tyrannical elephant.

Suddenly, an unexpected animal moved slowly to the front of the crowd. A hush accompanied the little animal's action, as no one expected him to say anything. All of the humans and animals were surprised to see the tortoise moving to the front like an animal with a mission.

The tortoise was one of the animals that went into exile. The small but shrewd animal had lived among the shrubs near the humans since he ran from the elephant. Everyone underrated the tortoise, but no one had a solution to the dilemma.

"Who are you, Little One?" asked the village chief.

"I'm *Ijapa T'iroko Oko Yannibo*, Your Highness," responded the tortoise. "May you wear the crown for so long, and may your sandals march the soil continually, Royal One. I pray that you bear the horse-tail whisker longer than your ancestors. I

The Hidden Treasures in Gray Hair

came with good news—I have a proposal for cutting the uncouth elephant to size."

No one was surprised when the village chief responded halfheartedly to Ijapa's proposal. Like everyone else, the chief did not expect the tortoise to possess any extraordinary power. He thought that the humans and the powerful animals had tried everything they could to no avail.

"With your permission, Your Royal Highness, I would bring the elephant's pride to an end shortly," Ijapa said with assurance.

The tortoise's motive remained unclear to both humans and animals. At best, they thought the tortoise was looking for a way to shore up his image. Little creatures sometimes aspire to do big things to sway positive opinions in their directions. That was what many of those present thought.

"How are you going to accomplish that, Ijapa?" the chief asked.

"Please, leave the details to me, your highness," retorted the tortoise. "I'll bring the boastful elephant to the village."

The chief was not convinced by the tortoise's assurance, but he decided to honor his request anyway. After all, he had nothing to lose if the elephant killed Ijapa. He was aware that the giant beast had killed several humans and many animals.

"I grant your request, Ijapa," said the chief, with little concern for the tortoise's wellbeing.

The tortoise requested the villagers to prepare an elaborate throne before he returned with the elephant. He asked them to dig a ditch in front of the throne, and place sharp objects in it. Additionally, he instructed them to cover the ditch with a well-decorated mat.

No one understood Ijapa's motive for the unusual requests, but they promised to comply. They had nothing to lose. Everyone was ready to do anything to stop the elephant from causing further problems. The village chief, in particular, was ready to do whatever it took, for normal life to return to the village.

The villagers started preparing according to Ijapa's specifications as soon as he departed the village to look for the elephant. They constructed a magnificent throne and decorated it with the latest accessories. They also dug a deep ditch and mounted upward-facing spears inside. Furthermore, they covered the ditch with a well-knitted mat.

Ijapa disappeared into the jungle to look for the bad-mannered elephant. He travelled across seven rivers and seven hills in search of the self-imposed king of the jungle. Everyone waited for him and the elephant to return to the village. It was the longest waiting for the villagers.

Sure enough, the tortoise located the elephant after a while. The boastful elephant had not changed a bit. He continued with his usual style of looking down on other animals. The elephant was

The Hidden Treasures in Gray Hair

even shouting orders to some animals as the tortoise arrived.

"Hey, you, gazelle, run down to the river and get me some water," the elephant commanded. The gazelle did as he was ordered, because no one dared play around when the elephant gave an instruction. The other animals looked down in fear, as they dared not look at the elephant straight in the eyes.

"Where have you been, Little One?" the elephant questioned Ijapa. "You and the other miserable animals disappeared for no good reasons. Now, you are back. I thought you won't ever return to the animal kingdom. Please, tell us what you want, the petite character."

"I came to deliver an important and urgent message to you, Your Royal Highness," responded the tortoise. "The humans sent a very interesting message to you." Ijapa bowed down before the elephant as he delivered the bizarre message. The elephant showed instant interest in the message, because he wanted to know what the humans thought of him.

"Tell me, *Ijapa T'iroko Oko Yannibo*. What do the humans want? Are they mad at me or do they fear me? I want to know immediately." The elephant became impatient. He wanted to know everything about the humans. He remembered that he killed some humans before, and he damaged their huts occasionally. However, he was not sure what they thought of him.

"I salute Your Highness, the giant who shakes the jungle inside out. I brought good news from the humans. They marveled at your raw power and wisdom. They wished they had someone like you among them, but they had none. Thus, they asked me to...."

"Tell me everything, right now! They wanted me to be their king?"The elephant was not patient for Ijapa to conclude his statement. He cut into his speech and gestured with his trunk for Ijapa to spill everything quickly. Deep inside, Ijapa was happy that the elephant was excited about the imaginary message he brought.

"Yes, Your Highness. The humans wanted you to come to their village. They wanted you to be their king, as they had nobody as powerful and smart to direct their affairs." Ijapa rolled out lines of sweet words that made the prideful elephant happy. He could tell that his trick was already working, as the elephant was interested in his statements.

"Are you sure the humans want me to be their king?" asked the elephant on a second thought. "The humans are smarter than I thought. They recognize that I had a lot to offer. That is so sweet of them. I think I'll accept their request, and go with you to the humans to become their king."

"I'm willing to present you to the humans, Your Royal Highness," said the tortoise as the other animals watched in amazement. They were pleased

The Hidden Treasures in Gray Hair

to hear that the elephant would leave the animal kingdom to become the king of the humans.

"We should be on our way immediately," the elephant beckoned the tortoise to lead the way. The self-made king of the jungle departed his subjects without saying goodbye to them. Ijapa led the way and the elephant followed as the two departed the animal kingdom.

The tortoise and the elephant travelled beyond the rivers and the hills. The long journey did not look far to the two animals. They were both excited for different reasons. Ijapa was happy that he would soon hold the elephant accountable for all of his irresponsible behaviors. The elephant was glad that he would not only be the king of the animal kingdom, he would also rule the humans.

The tortoise slowed down deliberately as the two animals neared the human village. He was able to put his planned tricks to use. The elephant, on the other hand, was full of energy. He wanted to arrive at the human village as soon as he could, so he could begin his reign of terror among the humans.

"Wouldn't it be nice if we arrive at the human village soon, so you could be crowned quickly, your highness?" Ijapa asked the elephant.

"You are right, Ijapa, but you are too slow for that to happen," responded the elephant.

"Well, I have a proposal," said Ijapa. "We are very close to the humans. We would even get to them quicker if your highness could carry me on your back, so we could move faster."

"Come on, hop on my back, the slow one," ordered the elephant. "That won't hurt me any bit. You are too small and light-weighted for me to feel anything," the huge beast said as he stooped down for the tortoise to climb on his back.

Ijapa secretly savored the laughter of his first victory over the boastful elephant. *The elephant brutalized me in the past. Now, I'm riding him like a horse,* he thought, as he sat comfortably on the back of the king of the plains. The two animals were very close to the humans then.

The elephant and the tortoise soon arrived at the humans' village. The village chief and his subjects, who had been expecting the two animals for some time, could not believe their eyes. They were amazed that Ijapa did not only bring the elephant to the village, as he promised, but even rode on his back, as he sang:

We'll make elephant the king
Let the festivity begin
We'll make elephant the king
Let the festivity begin

Ijapa crooned, as the two animals neared the splendid throne. True to his nature, the boastful elephant approached the royal chair without prompting. He started thinking of what to say to the humans immediately he climbed the throne. Unfortunately, the tortoise had a different idea.

The Hidden Treasures in Gray Hair

"Set me down, Your Royal Majesty," requested the little animal. "I cannot ride on your back as you approach the throne. You'll become the king of the whole wide world as soon as you set your feet on that throne. I mean you would rule both the humans and the animals," Ijapa said. The elephant went down on his knees immediately and set him down.

"To the pleasure of the humans and the animals, I present to you the king of all living things, King Elephant the Great!" the crafty tortoise said as he gestured the elephant toward the glittering royal stool. The humans and the animals clapped and danced in expectation of what would follow. Unfortunately for the elephant, he had no clue what would happen next. He thought everyone was pleased to see him become the extraordinary king.

Full of inordinate pride to the end, the elephant fell into the covered ditch as he took the first step toward the throne. He fell on the hidden spears and they pierced his body. The village hunters went to work immediately. They speared the disrespectful elephant till he stopped wincing.

Chapter 8
RESPECT—The Rebounding Reward

Like a boomerang, respect keeps coming back when you throw it at others. People respect you when you respect them; just as you get something back, when you give to others.

———————————————

The child who looks at his mother rudely
Would be bankrupt for life
The child who looks at his father rudely
Would be bankrupt for life
The mother who labored to have you
The father who struggled to raise you
The child who looks at his mother rudely
Would be bankrupt for life

I thought that was the most popular song as I grew up. Then, I heard another one, still praising the mother:

Mother is the jewel of immeasurable value
I cannot buy one with money

*She nurtured me in the womb for nine months
And carried me on her back for three years
Mother is the jewel of immeasurable value
I cannot buy one with money*

The students grinned from ear to ear as they sang these songs. They sprang on their feet and swung their arms proudly while they marched to their classrooms. Youth took the songs seriously, as every child appeared to mean every word in them. The level of respect for parents had no bounds.

Respect was like a synonym for "parent." Children respected and celebrated their parents like little gods across the land. Children were easily irritated when people said negative things about their parents. The boys prostrated and the girls knelt down in the morning to greet their parents. The parents offered them blessings in return.

"Get up from the ground, my son! Hope you woke up well, one-of-a-kind child. You'll be lucky today," responded my grandmother and grandfather when I greeted them in the morning. I cherished the blessings that I received from my grandparents before I headed to my daily chores. I thought it was better to receive little words of prayer from the adults than the little words that could set one back in life.

I did not look far before I discovered that parents deserved respect from their children. I found all of the evidences I needed in my own home. My grandparents proved it to me many times over. I

The Hidden Treasures in Gray Hair

watched Grandma serve me the last food in the house after school. She would sit and watch me eat, even when she had nothing to eat herself.

Although I requested her to eat some of the food with me, Grandma would smile and encourage me to eat everything by myself. She was probably making up for her inability to give me lunch money for school.

"I'd rather go hungry than for you to be half full, my son," said my grandmother with a smile on her face. Perhaps that was the least among the pains she took on my behalf. She did far too much for me to recount everything. I would rather tell the story of my grandmother's love for me throughout my lifetime.

I could not forget my grandfather's affection, too. He did a lot for me, and some of the things he did keep rebounding in my memory. Grandpa departed to the great beyond decades ago, but I will never stop loving and respecting him for the outstanding things he did for me.

My grandfather carried me on his shoulders as we crossed the *Okoo* Stream on the way to the farm. The stream was usually full beyond the log bridge on it during the raining season, and young children were no match for the boisterous stream. *Grandpa won't let this stream carry me away*, I thought.

I would be kidding if I thought carrying me across the stream was the best Grandpa could do for me. He did something greater than that on the same day. He was spraying his cocoa trees to guard against pests. He did that annually, like the other cocoa farmers. The mixed-chemical container hung on his back as he moved the pump's handle up and down with his left hand, and held the sprayer nozzle with his right hand.

I sat at a nearby clearing and watched my grandfather caring for his cash crop. Grandma and *Oga Imisi* were fetching water and mixing the chemicals. Then, the horrifying incident that followed made me think that my grandfather loved me as much as my grandmother.

I let out a sharp cry when an ant bit me. My grandfather yanked the chemical pump off of his back and thundered toward me. "What happened!?" he asked passionately, ready to do justice to whatever messed with his little grandson. He found the culprits as soon as he looked around me. A couple of ants were on the ground.

Grandpa looked at me carefully to make sure there were no ants hanging on me. Then, he carried me to another spot where there were no ants. He made sure I was okay before he returned to the pump, only to find out that it was broken. I was unhappy that my grandfather's pump was damaged because of me.

"Don't worry about it, son. You are far more precious than the pump," Grandpa said, without a dint of regret in his voice. I knew he meant every word he said at that moment. That occasion made me think that people should sing for the fathers as much as they did for the mothers.

There were fewer songs for fathers (and grandfathers), but people justified the endless songs for mothers. They reasoned that mothers' love was endless for their children. That's why people composed more songs for the mothers. One more popular mother's song kept reminding me of what my grandmother did, so I could be happy:

Mother is my surety
She raised me from infancy
With her back, she carried me
Good job, I say to my mother
I salute my mother for all she did
With so much respect, I hail you, Mother
Never would I refuse errands for my mother
Never! Never!! Never!!!

People sang about mothers beyond the schools. They praised them everywhere, including places of work and worship. Everyone seemed to have some words of respect for mothers.

Respect was not limited to parents only. Reverence was universal among the *Yorubas*. Youths were taught to respect the other members of their families, including uncles, aunties, brothers, sisters, cousins, nephews, nieces, and others.

Series of popular sayings reminded people to treat their homes (families) with respect, because home was the last result. One such saying included, "One returns home to rest after a hard day's work." Another one stated, "A ship returns home to dock after sailing the seas and the lagoons."

We were told that the home (family) was the last refuge if others rejected us. The youth were advised to be nice to all but to revere their families, because the latter were the only people left if others rejected them.

"Friends may reject you when worldly turbulence rages, but your family will shelter you," they said. That was not in any way meant to belittle friendship, but to make one remember his family just as he cares about his friends. That is, one should be as nice and connected with his family as he is to his friends.

Youths were trained to respect other adults in sight, in addition to their parents and the elderly members of their families. The youths respected other adults, even when they were not related. Younger people called older males *Oga*, and the older females *Anti*. The youths called elderly males who were old enough to be their fathers *Baba*, and the elderly females *Mama*, regardless of whether they were related or not.

The youths took delight in respecting all adults that came their ways so that the next generation of younger people could respect them when they grew up. There was an infectious belief that respect was a boomerang. Adults told reverent youths that their good manners would come back to them someday. They said younger people would respect them, too, later in their lives. Respect was

The Hidden Treasures in Gray Hair

seen in terms of the harvest that followed a planting season. All looked forward to harvesting the respect they sowed.

The youths respected other people's parents like they respected their own. They treated other people's brothers, sisters, aunties, and uncles the same way they treated theirs. That explained why the *Yorubas* addressed family friends, neighbors, and acquaintances the same way they addressed their own families.

For instance, *Yoruba* youths sometimes addressed elderly family friends, neighbors, or acquaintances as daddies, mummies, uncles, or aunties, as the case may be. That was because the *Yorubas* respected and treated others the same way they treated their own.

The adults taught the youths to respect everyone, regardless of whether they liked them or not. They said respect was not about affection, but about "live and let live." The adults maintained that respect had to do with showing tolerance and being sensitive to other people's feelings.

Society mandated the youths to respect the authority and those in positions of authority. They requested that young people respect public properties. The adults taught the youths to revere their nation, culture, and beliefs. Additionally, they told them to respect themselves.

The elders had good reasons for teaching the youths to respect all, including themselves. The adults insisted that respect should start from individuals, just as charity began at home. They wanted people to respect themselves, because those who did not respect themselves would not respect others.

The youths tried to respect themselves by doing the appropriate things. They embraced the pillars of character, including respect, responsibility, citizenship, caring, fairness, and trustworthiness. The golden rule of treating others the way they wanted to be treated became important to youths.

The adults believed that those who respected neither themselves nor others would not respect their nation and culture. In the end, those who had no respect for others were not counted as good citizens. People saw them as appalling citizens because they lacked responsibility for their nation and did not care about fellow citizens.

On the other hand, people trusted and appreciated those who respected others. Respectful individuals were considered to be civic and dependable people. They earned other people's admiration and goodwill. People tried to find ways to return the good gestures of those who respected them.

I have a memorable narrative to prove that people get something back when they respect others. I received something for respecting my teachers. The "gift" that I received helped me thereafter and I still have it with me today. Mr. Olorunfemi, the Integrated Science teacher, said I de-

The Hidden Treasures in Gray Hair

served something for respecting teachers and fellow students. He gave me his personal formula for remembering the first twenty atomic elements.

"You are a very respectful student," began the teacher. "I will teach you something that might benefit you in the future. Is it easy for you to recount the first twenty elements on the periodic table?"

"It is a little difficult, sir. I'm yet to master them," I responded. The teacher spoke with my class about the "atomic elements" a couple of days earlier. He said there were many elements, but he requested us to memorize the first twenty elements.

"*Hi Helen, Let Big Boys Come Near Our Farm. Newly Sociable Mr. Allen Sent Peter Some Cows Around Popular Camp.*" Mr. Olorunfemi said audibly as he recounted his personal memory aid, for remembering the first twenty atomic elements. He wrote them on a piece of paper and handed it to me.

"Here, memorize this. It will help you someday," said the teacher as he handed me the paper. "I've been thinking of what to offer you for being so respectful. You will spend money if I give you some, but you will remember this for a long time. Who knows, you might need it someday."

"Thank you, sir," I thanked the teacher for the unique gift. I was delighted that I would no longer struggle to recall the first twenty atomic elements—hydrogen, helium, lithium, beryllium, boron, carbon, nitrogen, oxygen, fluorine, neon, sodium, magnesium, aluminum, silicon, phosphorus, sulfur, chlorine, argon, potassium, and calcium.

Mr. Olorunfemi vacated the class for another teacher a few weeks after that, but the exceptional gift he gave me did not leave. The memory aid he'd offered became useful as soon as a new teacher took over, very close to the examination. The new teacher actually asked us to write down the first twenty atomic elements. I passed that examination in flying colors. I harvested the respect I sowed earlier on.

People told many memorable folktales about respect. Once upon a time, there was a fierce famine in the animal kingdom. The fields were dried and there was not a single grain for the animals to eat. Everyone was hungry and miserable.

The famine was so bad that it bred indiscipline among the animals. The young animals assumed that the adults had failed them by not providing food. They could not understand that the adults tried their best, but Mother Nature sometimes defied living things' efforts. Thus, they started disrespecting their adults.

"Who do you think you are—a deity?" That was a little cub talking to his father. "You can't order me around when you can't even provide food for the family."

The Hidden Treasures in Gray Hair

"Leave me alone," a young elephant told her mother. "Whose life is it anyway? I have to fend for myself somehow. You can't feed me, after all."

"Stop it! Don't tell me what to do," a young giraffe nagged her mother as the mother counseled her against being careless when playing near a lion's den. "You are tall and I'm tall as well. Is there something you have that I don't have? Do you know something that I don't know?"

Aja, the dog, was the only animal who respected his mother. His father had died a couple of years earlier. The dog revered his mother so much that he would do anything to protect her. He did not allow anyone to disrespect her. *Aja* was there for his mother when she needed him.

The famine became harsher in the animal kingdom. The animals expected things to turn around, but the hard times became tougher. The resentments between the young and the old animals grew worse. However, all of the animals agreed on something. They understood they had to do something to remain alive.

"A serious ailment requires a serious medication," said the king of the animals. "We have to do something tough, else we won't survive. There won't be new generations of animals to take our places when we die."

The animals held meetings for days, trying to find a far-reaching solution to the problem. Eventually, an animal suggested that the animals should eat their mothers. She reasoned that the younger animals would survive and rear the future generations of animals. The animal added that the older animals would die anyway if the younger ones did not eat them. That was a strange suggestion, but all of the animals agreed to it.

An overwhelming majority of the animals showed no emotion about eating their own mothers. They had no regards for their mothers after all. The dog was the only animal that refused the suggestion to eat his mother. He preferred to starve than eat his mother.

The powerful animals, including elephant, lion, tiger, leopard, jaguar, lynx, caracal, and cheetah ate their mothers. The weaker animals, like the antelope, goat, cat, and tortoise ate their mothers, too. Soon, all the animals had eaten their mothers, except the dog. *Aja* did not allow anything to happen to his mother.

The dog carried his mother to heaven and hid her behind the clouds. The other animals wondered where *Aja's* mother was, because nobody saw him eating her. They pestered *Aja* with many questions about his mother's whereabouts.

"I'm sorry to inform you that my mother died a few days ago," began the dog. "I buried her because I didn't feel like eating her. I guess she should be in heaven now."

"Sorry for losing your mother that way, *Aja*," said the animals in unison.

"You did the right thing. You respected your mother by burying her, instead of eating her. We

The Hidden Treasures in Gray Hair

should have thought of a better solution to the famine, instead of eating our mothers," the king of animals said.

The idea of eating one's mother became immoral to the animals, and they decided to put an end to it. They realized that they could have thought of a better solution, instead of what they did. The animals decided to look for food in other ways, instead of engaging in cannibalism.

It was time for the dog to savor the bliss of keeping his mother while the other animals ate theirs. As the other animals struggled to find food, Aja secretly went to his mother in heaven to eat. He started looking robust when the other animals looked miserable. Some animals, including the tortoise, began to wonder how Aja managed to look so good.

The tortoise woke up at dawn one day and hid near Aja's house. He wanted to find out where the full-bodied animal found food. Soon, Aja came out of his house and started walking toward a deserted part of the town. The tortoise followed him unnoticed from a distance.

The dog looked toward the heaven at a particular point and started singing an unusual song:

Mother, spin down the rope
Chorus: Alujanjankijan
Mother, spin down the rope
All animals ate their mothers
The elephant ate his mother
The buffalo ate his mother

The lion ate his mother
But the dog carried his to heaven
Mother, spin down the rope

The heavens opened up as soon as the dog concluded his song, and a rope dropped down to the earth. The dog climbed the rope to heaven and disappeared into the clouds. He returned after a while with different types of food. Aja returned home without realizing that the tortoise had seen everything he did. As usual, the dog continued to live happily.

Unknown to the dog, the tortoise went to the spot where the former climbed to the heaven the previous day. The tortoise sang the dog's song, and the rope descended to the earth. Soon, the tortoise started climbing toward the clouds.

"This is easy! I don't have to worry about the famine anymore," the tortoise said to himself as he climbed. "I could come here whenever the dog is not around and take food home for my family."

Unfortunately for the tortoise, *Aja* appeared suddenly. The dog could not believe what he saw. He witnessed the tortoise ascending into the clouds. He knew immediately that the crafty animal was trying to double-cross him. The dog would not take any of the swindling.

"Why should someone who disrespected and ate his mother come to mine for food," the dog asked himself. He knew what to do instantly. Aja started singing the song in reverse order, to undo what the tortoise was doing:

The Hidden Treasures in Gray Hair

> *Mother, slash the rope*
> *Chorus: Alujanjankijan*
> *Mother, slash the rope*
> *All animals ate their mothers*
> *The elephant ate his mother*
> *The buffalo ate his mother*
> *The lion ate his mother*
> *But the dog carried his to heaven*
> *Mother, slash the rope*

The dog's mother recognized her son's voice and slashed the rope from above. The tortoise came crashing down to the parched earth. He was alive, but his shell was badly broken.

The news of what happened went round the town so fast. The animals learned something from how Aja's respect for his mother saved him from hunger. They also learned that the tortoise, who had disrespected and eaten his mother, harvested something awful in return.

"No one should disrespect his parents," counseled the king of the animals. "It is immoral to disrespect the adults. As a matter of fact, it is depraving to disrespect anyone. It is shortsighted individuals who disrespect others. Henceforth, everyone should respect and tolerate others."

Chapter 9
TOLERANCE— The Exploit of the Broadminded

Acceptance is not everyone's business, as it should be. It is an ideal embraced only by the open-minded. Narrow-minded individuals are too shortsighted to see the benefits of tolerance.

Like most toddlers elsewhere, I was a very innocent child. I knew very little about the world. I even thought the world began and ended in the town I was born. I had no idea there was another world elsewhere. The town was the only universe I knew. Consequently, I discovered or heard something new about the world almost every day as I grew up.

Exploring and discovering new things seemed like the most rewarding part of my life at that point. People knew that I loved to unearth new things. However, nobody thought I was up to something fresh one beautiful morning, when I was left to gaze at the skies outside the house. The urge to discover something new about the world dug into my mind, and I could not resist it.

I noticed the large golden sun inching its way up the eastern horizon. The astonishing glory of the sun appeared to be rising from the ground and climbing up the sky. The initially huge sun became smaller as it slowly climbed into the sky over the houses in the distance. I thought the sky enveloped my town. The heavens appeared to enclose the town at some equidistance from where I stood.

There is no harm in walking the distance and touching the sky where it meets the ground, I thought. *It would be amazing to see the hole from which the sun emerged a while ago before climbing into the skies.*

Accordingly, I started moving toward the direction where the sun came up that morning. That was supposed to be my first exploration of the wide, wild, and willful world beyond the neighborhood where I lived. I was ecstatic that I was about to discover where the sun came out of the ground before it climbed into the sky in its daily journey above my town.

Little did I realize that there was more to the earth than my naked eyes could see. The closer I thought I was to the place where the ground met the sky, the farther the sky moved away from me. Regardless, I refused to give up, because I did not want to quit. I kept moving toward my newest discovery.

Eventually, I became disoriented and got lost at an unknown part of the town. I gave up the idea of seeing where the sky and the ground met, and turned back. I thought the new challenge of retracing my footsteps back home would be easier, but I was wrong. The more I tried to figure out my way, the deeper I got lost into new neighborhoods.

So, the world is larger than I thought, I started thinking.

In the end, I stood at a street corner and cried. I knew that someone would help me shortly. I had been told to keep away from strangers, but I realized that I had to trust a stranger at that point. I thought I had to keep on crying till a caring adult asked me what the matter was. I believed that whoever responded to me would be a kind and trustworthy person. I expected something new to happen, as usual.

Mama Talabi, my great aunty, showed up shortly. She was at the right place at the right time. She recognized me instantly, and took me home to my worried grandmother, who was already looking for me.

That was the innocence of a child in action. Children in my town took things at their face value without chewing over their complexities. Young people were straightforward, basic, tolerant, and trusting. They had no grudges against people on the basis of their ethnicity, race, or religion. Clear as morning dew, children appeared as the purest members of society.

As a toddler, I smiled at whoever smiled at me. I opened my arms and embraced whoever embraced me. I did not bear grudge against any race, and I saw no lines between cultures. I had no reason to resent another child because his religion was different from mine. The diverse religions appeared to me like assorted ways of worshipping the only God. Apparently, prejudices did not belong to toddlers' world, till the adults, circumstances, and events around them started saying otherwise.

I was (and am) a Christian and I had friends in the diverse religions. I knew people who embraced the local deities, and I even had associates who had no religion at all. The other children and I welcomed the members of the other races who visited our town without making derogatory distinctions about their races and skin colors.

"*Oyinbo!*" We would hail and socialize with the white visitors, using the local name for light-skinned people.

I have discovered a lot more about mankind and the world since. I have found out there are more towns in addition to my hometown. I have discovered that ethnic groups coexist as nations. I know that the United Nations Organization, UNO, is made up of many countries.

The Hidden Treasures in Gray Hair

I understand that the world comprises of several continents, including North America, South America, Europe, Africa, Asia, Australia, and the Antarctica. I know that our solar system comprises of planets, including Mercury, Venus, Earth, Mars, Jupiter, Saturn, Uranus, Neptune, and Pluto (though that was later downsized to a smaller heavenly body).

From A to Z, I now know more about the world. From Afghanistan to Zimbabwe, I am aware that the world is stunningly beautiful. I have seen the imposing prairies of North America, the scenic plateaus of Africa, and the rolling hills of Europe. I admire the thrilling waters of the Caribbean, the truly amazing forests of the Amazon in South America, and the beautiful snows of Greenland.

I have learned about the meandering rivers of Asia, the photo-finish harbors of Australia, and the awe-inspiring sand dunes of the Middle East. The continental ice of the Antarctica is a marvel to me. The enthralling beauties of the earth seem endless.

Unfortunately, I have also learned that the diverse peoples of the world mistrust one another, in spite of the stunning world. The diverse peoples are yet to have complete faith in one another after centuries of civilization. Mankind continues to try, but not everyone has figured out that we share the same heritages, and our destinies are intertwined.

Mankind has fought many wars, but tolerance remains the single war that we must wage and win. Then, we could savor the breathtaking beauty of the earth. Regrettably, people sometimes limit themselves to their own cultures, beliefs, and religions, and end up shutting themselves away from the rest of the world.

Those who limit themselves know little about others. Those who know little about others are ignorant of others' ways of life, cultures, and beliefs. Uninformed individuals fear other cultures, and they end up not tolerating others. People would tolerate one another more if we try to understand one another. All of mankind should be free to explore the different parts of the world without fear.

Some people are not comfortable with discussions on race, but that amounts to avoiding the reality. Mankind's bitter past makes race discussions difficult, but we cannot shun the actuality. We could only avoid discussing race to the peril of the coming generations. People would make the old mistakes if they do not know what happened in the past.

Like a book, the world has to be read. An ignorant person who limits himself to his own culture is like the person who reads a single page from the book. A tolerant person who devotes time to learning about others is like the one who reads the whole book. Tolerant people end up knowing more, and they are better equipped about the world.

The Hidden Treasures in Gray Hair

Some people use almost everything that is different about others against them. Such include race, skin color, ethnicity, nationality, gender, religion, language, social class, physical appearance, and more. They sometimes make up things to isolate people into groups. People occasionally seek common grounds with those who look like them, so they could exclude others. It takes open-minded people to avoid using common grounds in such a way.

Diversity is beautiful if we look at its advantages and not the challenges it comes with. Like every good thing, diversity has its own hitches. However, its advantages outweigh its disadvantages. Mankind would be stronger if we accumulate the strengths, ideas, talents, and resources of the diverse peoples of our planet. We could overcome most of the challenges of diversity if we permit compromises. People are unique, but we could avoid stepping on each other's toes if we respect and tolerate one another.

My grandmother talked to me about open-mindedness. As a teenager, I heard people demeaning other ethnic groups, but Grandma wanted me to see the whole world as my constituency. She overheard some kids making unwarranted ethnic jokes one day, and she asked if I was one of them. Grandma was pleased that I was opposed to such jokes.

"Those who make disparaging jokes about other cultures are narrow-minded people," said

Grandma."They don't understand the benefits of diversity. What unites the whole of mankind is far more than what separates them."

I could not resist every chance I had to speak with my grandparents. They were full of wisdom about many things that interested me. I learned something interesting every time I spoke with the two elderly people. They were my replenishing sources of wisdom.

"The red blood inside the members of your ethnic group is what is inside the members of other ethnic groups. Though tongues and clans may be different, all of mankind is basically the same," my grandmother explained.

"People from the diverse ethnic groups won't have similar flesh, blood, bones, and others if they were not physically related. Normally, every human being, regardless of race, culture, or religion, has one head, two eyes, two ears, two hands, and two legs."

I was glad to share another thoughtful moment with my grandmother. I thought I should grab the opportunity to tell her about my own take on tolerance. I knew that I shared her feelings about human relations. I understood she would be glad to know that her grandchild agreed with her belief—that all of mankind was one.

"People should realize that nobody chooses his or her race," I said. "I think we all found ourselves where we found ourselves."

The Hidden Treasures in Gray Hair

"A black man did not choose his race by himself," my grandmother agreed, "and a white woman did not select her clan either. Nature branded each of us the skin color it chose." I perfectly understood what she was saying. That was the beauty of dialoguing with an insightful adult.

"That means anyone could have been African, European, American, Asian, Caribbean, Indian, Jewish, or Arab," I said, remembering to mention the diverse peoples I learned in Social Studies class a couple of weeks earlier.

"You are right, son. People belonged to the races that providence chose for them."

"I know that children take after their parents," I said, "but the children don't determine their races or skin colors themselves. They find themselves where they find themselves. Why do people detest each other, when race is just a game of chance?"

"It is the same with religion," Grandma changed to faith. "Many people practice their parents' religions. Others simply practice the one the people around them practice. Many practice those religions, not necessarily because they chose them on their own. Then, why would anyone hate another because of the religion passed on by another person?"

"Family, nationality, persuasion, personal conviction, and circumstances influence people's choices of religion," I summarized. "The Pope's sister is inclined to be a Catholic and the son of Mecca's Grand Imam would likely be a Muslim."

"I'm impressed! You are a smart young man," my grandmother said, as she stared at me astonishingly.

"I wouldn't say I'm smarter than many people out there. Everybody should understand the logic that nobody chose his race before he came into this world," I reasoned out loud.

"It takes a smart person to understand and abide by that logic," Grandma insisted. "There are people who should understand that nobody created himself. Such people erroneously assume that they are supporting their races, religions, or cultures when they show prejudices against others."

The evening was far spent, but I had no regrets speaking with my grandmother. I did not lose anything by not discussing petty things with the neighborhood kids down at the playground. I was having fun, discussing a philosophical issue with my wisdom-laden grandmother.

"Those who detest others to show they love their race have no idea what love is," she said firmly. "It is those who cannot stand on their own who mischievously tie themselves to their races' aprons. Those who could bear their own weights are not afraid to mingle with the diverse world."

"I wonder why the world continues to advance in knowledge, but not in getting along," I chipped in.

The Hidden Treasures in Gray Hair

"Humanity seems to understand war more than peace. Mankind has fought two big wars. And it has been wars without end since. Millions of innocent children, defenseless women, and devoted fathers have perished in wars they knew nothing about," Grandma explained.

"Who is going to make the world a better place?" I asked in complete frustration.

"People like you, of course. My generation is old. We would count on your generation to reconcile the world by building bridges between cultures."

I wondered why my grandmother thought I had something that would make people stop bigotry and get along with one another.

"How could I stop intolerance and make the people around the world get along?" I questioned. "Is it possible for one person to unite the different races? Could I possibly bond the diverse faiths in the world? I'm just a kid. I'm not even the president of a nation."

"You don't even have to be one of the president's staff before you could make a difference," Grandma said with a smile. I waited for the elderly woman to teach me how to make the world a better place.

"It is simple," began Grandma. "You could make a difference by doing your part. It starts with doing unto others what you want them to do to you. Don't speak ill of other cultures. Be open-minded about the other races. Do not accept the disparaging things said by others till you witness them yourself. Don't fight with someone because his ancestors offended your ancestors. Then, you could turn an opponent to a supporter someday."

Grandma was right. Circumstances proved her right many years after she challenged me to make the world a better place. A number of events happened years after her advice, and how I resolved them made me feel like I made a difference. Recounting a few of those events would show how right my grandmother was.

One of the events happened when I graduated from college. There was a mandatory one-year national youth service. Young college graduates were posted to the different parts of the country. The program was meant to familiarize youth with the other parts of the country. The nation was made up of many subgroups.

I was posted to one of the states where the dominant ethnic group was known as *Igbo*. For my part, I was glad to be posted to that part of the country, because my *Igbo* friends were nice on campus. I revealed my joy to everyone who listened to me. Regrettably, I did not realize that someone was opposed to my gusto.

"I hope they won't eat you before you return to this part of the world," an uneducated man in my neighborhood joked.

The Hidden Treasures in Gray Hair

"That's an offensive joke!" I chided. "Please, don't repeat it. I attended school with some *Igbos*, and they were some of the most civilized students on campus. Why would anyone make such distasteful joke about them?"

The *Igbos* were very accepting. They embraced and lived in every part of the country. They were also some of the most industrious people in the country. Personally, I felt offended that someone made such an unfounded joke about the harmless people.

"I'm sorry; I didn't intend to hurt your feelings," the man replied, on noticing how upset I was. "Someone from that part of the country made the same joke about my ethnicity when I travelled there some years ago." He attempted to justify the unsolicited shaggy-dog story.

"Don't make uncharitable jokes about a people because someone from that group made jokes about your group in the past," I preached. "Every group has its own bad eggs, after all. Don't speak ill of another group because of its bad eggs. Be open-minded about the other cultures."

"You are right; that was an outrageous joke in the first place. I will be more sensitive to other ethnicities next time," the man promised.

I travelled to the heart of *Igbo* land thereafter and spent my national service year with some of the most welcoming people in that country. The *Igbos* made me feel at home, and I still feel like one of them many years after. My grandmother was right. Do not accept the disparaging things said by others till you witness them yourself. Also, do not make uncharitable jokes about a people because someone from that group made jokes about your group in the past.

Someone may ask why he has to be nice to the group whose members did bad things to his people in the past. The answer is simple. Some members of that group probably objected to the ill done by their members. It is fair to be nice to the group, at least, for the sake of the good ones. The *Yorubas* say that the pet owner who leaves water in the yard for his pet does not do so because of the stray lizards that drink from the water. He leaves the water because of his pet.

Another event corroborated my grandmother's advice about ethnic issues. Remember, she cautioned me not to fight with someone because his ancestors offended my ancestors. Grandma opined that I could turn an opponent to a supporter if I was open-minded. That happened during my sojourn in a neighboring country years after.

I was taking a walk in the evening when a car knocked down a pedestrian. The driver was white; the pedestrian was black. The young man on foot was in a haste to join his friends across the road, without doing so at the crosswalk. The pedestrian fell down and sustained some bruises. The development upset his friends, and they tried to fight with the driver.

I should point to the fact that the people of that country were very pleasant, as they loved visitors and treated them with respect. However, it was not unusual for a handful of individuals to be different from the mainstream people of a nation.

"You wan' kill my brother because he be black?" questioned the muscular leader of the group in broken English. *"Slave trade time don pass,"* he added as some Good Samaritans assisted the slightly bruised pedestrian.

Justifiably, many Africans, including myself, were outraged by the transatlantic slave trade that ravaged the continent some centuries ago. However, an overwhelming majority of the people were forgiving and looking up to a better future instead. It was unusual for people to provoke fights in the street because of the bitter past.

Obviously, the driver did not knock down the pedestrian purposefully. I understood the feelings of the youth who were unhappy with the past, but most Africans would not carry lights and search for a fight on that basis. The people of Africa knew that a well-defined wronged party would not remain if they retaliated against the inhumane and exploitative slave trade indiscreetly.

We cannot bury the history, but we should never allow the resulting anger to create further problems for the coming generations, I thought.

My heart thumped and my breath quickened as the young men approached the driver. The daring young men that I was about to confront intimidated me, but I preferred to stand by the facts. I knew I had to do something unconventional to defend the innocent driver.

"I will ensure that all of you go to jail if you do anything to the driver," I said, dipping a hand inside my pocket and bringing out the little recorder that I carried with me most of the time. I had always believed that reporters should carry recorders around, because a story would not wait for people when it broke. I clicked something on the recorder and pretended it was a walkie-talkie.

"Yeah, Police Commander Boateng..." I started talking to an imaginary police officer. I believed that a hard-hitting ailment required a matching panacea. I realized that talking softly to the youth would not ease their tone.

I looked intently at the leader of that group as I spoke. Apparently, I was getting his attention. The man, who was very bold moments ago, began to tone down his menacing impression. The development assured me that I was in charge of the situation. The ringleader's hard glare melted into an attentive gaze.

"You dey support Obroni against your black brothers?" the man suggested tenderly.

"The fact that I stopped my brothers from doing wrong indicates that I would stop anyone from doing wrong. I would do the same if the driver tried to fight with you unjustifiably," I corrected the erroneous impression made by the young man.

The Hidden Treasures in Gray Hair

Whoever wants a solution without becoming a part of the problem should tackle racial issues honestly. Anyone who sides with his or her group subjectively without considering the facts is a part of the problem. I thought it was honorable to admit when my group erred, if I wanted the other group to admit when they wronged my group.

"*He be secret policeman,*" the ringleader whispered as he and his followers withdrew.

The visibly shaken driver was relieved instantly. He was surprised that I stood up for the facts, even when his opponents and I shared the same race and skin color.

"Tackle prejudices regardless of the color of the people involved," I advised. "Wouldn't you support an innocent black man if troublesome white youths try to attack him unjustifiably?" I asked the man.

"Now, I would. I must confess—I probably didn't do as much for a black man in my country. But I'm so impressed now to see a black man taking a big risk for me. I will remember what you did if my own people try to maltreat a black person," the man promised as I said goodbye to him. I recalled that my grandmother said I could turn an opponent to a supporter if I remained open-minded about the past.

It appeared like Grandma saw the future when another event substantiated the advice she gave me many years earlier. The latest event gave me the impression that lies may change, but the truth remains constant forever. Grandma's belief that one could turn an opponent to a supporter by being open-minded came to pass in another event.

I was new in the United States when the third event occurred. The *buba* and *sokoto* I wore while waiting for the bus gave me away as a newly arrived African. I dressed in the native attire to show my new friends how men dressed in my country.

Two white teenagers drove by as I sat at the bus stop. The passenger stuck his middle finger out of the car window and yelled, "N——-, go home!" I was shocked by what happened, but I knew that all whites were not like the youngsters. I was on my way shortly when the bus arrived. I could not stop thinking about why people show prejudices toward one another for no good reasons.

As providence would have it, the two teenagers were buying gas by the bus stop where I stopped. I approached them calmly without betraying my emotion. The boys looked guilty as they saw me coming. I wished they knew I was about to test my grandmother's hypothesis once again.

"Why did you call me name when I didn't offend you, and you didn't even know me?" I asked the youngsters calmly. The teenagers appeared relieved when they found out that I came in peace. The original culpable looks on their faces gave way to childish grins as they struggled for the right words to tell me.

The Hidden Treasures in Gray Hair

"I'm really sorry. I shouldn't have said that," the boy who called me the name apologized profusely. "I feel so bad to have said that to a gentleman like you," he added.

"No one deserves to be treated that way, but I forgive you," I said to the youngsters.

"My conscience is worrying me right now... I thought you were going to fight when you approached us, but you surprised me by being nice. From now on, I promise to be nice to those who are different than me," the boy said with a sincere look on his face.

The resolution was satisfactory to me. My grandmother's theory came to pass once again! Inordinate anger and the use of violence do not resolve misunderstanding among groups. Violence only breeds more violence. You can turn an opponent to an ally if you remain open-minded and apply discipline over an issue that upsets you.

Chapter 10
DISCIPLINE—
The Exceptional Endowment

Like a pack of slipshod swimmers in the open sea, people without discipline drift aimlessly in society. The tides carry them south when they should be heading north. Talent expires, beauty fades, and success fritters away without discipline.

"I would have graduated from the university, had a good job, and visited the whole world at the age of thirty-five—America, Europe, Asia, Australia...I would have had my own business, mansion, and cars. My children would be the best-dressed among their peers. I could even be the nation's president at that age." That was Fun'yo, sharing her innocent vision during the summer holiday.

Every student looked forward to the summer break. That was when youths gathered according to the groups they belonged to, and enjoyed the long break from school. No more teachers telling us what to do; homework was gone for that season; bells no longer set the limit for our daily chores; and the regimented school semester was over for a while. With euphoria, students would sing the memorable song as they looked forward to the holiday:

> *Holiday is coming*
> *Holiday is coming*
> *No more morning bells*
> *No more teachers' whip*
> *Goodbye teachers*
> *Goodbye scholars*
> *Now, we're going to have*
> *A jolly holiday*

The summer break meant something different, and many of us took full advantage of it. The youth engaged in diverse activities—we played different games and soccer, discussed the latest fashion trend, and talked about the future. Some kids went to the farm with their parents. Some travelled to other towns to visit relatives. Others just sat with friends and talked about their dreams for the future.

Fun'yo had all it took to go to college, graduate on top of her class, get a great job, travel the whole world, and even become the president, based on her dream. The girl was outstanding in several ways. She was intellectually gifted and visibly stylish. Fun'yo was the attractive town-girl that every boy wanted to date. People often associated her with the cliché of "brain, brawn, and beauty."

Everyone took Fun'yo's aspirations seriously. There was no basis for anyone to doubt her vision, when kids were kidding around and guessing where they would be in years to come. I expected Fun'yo's dream to come to pass someday, if she remained the town's well sought-after girl she was.

Fun'yo went through high school unscathed under her parents' keen supervision. However, her parents' eagle-eyes could not watch her for the rest of her life. She needed to make her own choices as she grew up and moved on to the university. Surprisingly, she lacked the audacity to match her dream with the same level of discipline.

The erstwhile compliant girl, with "brain, brawn, and beauty," started throwing caution into the wind and doing things in her own way. Fun'yo's lifestyle changed soon after she entered college. Her dream was to head north, but her approach to life headed south. Fun'yo ended up throwing a cog in her own wheel of progress.

Some of the good things about Fun'yo ensnared her because she lost control over the new circumstances around her. A swarm of affluent male students mobbed her because of her beauty and elegance. Fun'yo tried to enjoy her newly found freedom, class, and association. She knew and addressed some of the silver-spoon-fed young men on campus by their first names.

Fun'yo started drinking and carousing the night with the young men and women in her new social class. A get-together was not up to taste if Fun'yo was not a guest there. Merry-making became her pastime, instead of pursuing the academic laurels her parents sent her to college to achieve.

Fun'yo, the gentle sheep that associated with the untamed dogs, ended up eating what wild dogs ate. The erstwhile aspiring and amenable Fun'yo started experimenting with drugs. Hangovers prevented her from attending classes a lot of the time. Everything added up in the end, as Fun'yo started failing her classes.

The attractive, graceful, and sociable Fun'yo became ill a couple of years after. The people outside her circle couldn't tell what happened to her. However, rumor had it that Fun'yo contracted the most dreaded disease, HIV. Regrettably, the gifted girl, who dreamed of seeing the world, having her own family, cars, and mansion by age thirty-five, did not make it to that age.

Like Fun'yo, Debisi had promising future early in his life. His parents were poor, but people believed that the talented boy would break the vicious circle of poverty in his family. He was one of the best students in his school, and he often scored the highest marks in some subjects. People thought that Debisi would secure a scholarship

The Hidden Treasures in Gray Hair

and soar through college without financial hardship.

Debisi was also a budding athlete. He demonstrated his sporty prowess at the school's annual sport competitions. Not many competitors could outrun him in the school. Teachers and students alike appreciated Debisi. He got away with some things that his peers were reprimanded for. The girls outdid one another so they could become Debisi's girlfriends.

Everything seemed to be working for Debisi, except that he lacked the discipline to manage his good fortune. The first hint of Debisi's lack of restraint revealed itself when he started disrespecting teachers. Debisi would sit haughtily, frown, roll his eyes, and talk back at teachers when they corrected his newly developed unrestrained behavior.

"This is a free world. I don't need anyone's advice. I can manage my life by myself. " Debisi would argue, so he could place anyone who tried to correct him at bay. The young man did not realize there was more to life than being a brilliant and out-of-control sportsperson.

Debisi no longer thought that anyone deserved respect from him, because he was so talented. He looked up to becoming a popular athlete and earning scholarship to the university. Pride took the position of humility in Debisi's life. He lost touch with reality as he looked at life in terms of what his physical competence could offer him.

He forgot that talents expired, good looks faded, and success frittered away without discipline.

The boy, once loved by all, started losing his good friends. He walked around the campus as if he was the one in charge of the school. Debisi joined the "popular" boys on campus. The all-the-rage group of boys was the most sophisticated at the school. As one would have thought, they hung around the popular girls to complement their group.

The popular boys rolled up their shirts' sleeves and shorts' brims against the school tenet. Their shirts' collars flapped up their necks instead of folding downward. The boys stuck wooden combs into their big hairdos when the school requested males to sport reasonable amounts of hair. Like the rest of the popular boys, Debisi's shorts were deliberately larger than specification. The popular girls were not left out in the showy outlook either. Their skirts were shorter and tighter than normal.

The popular boys often ditched school. They would roam around the surrounding farmlands, loiter in uncompleted buildings near the school, or swim in a local watercourse. The boys and the girls smoked cigarettes and drank local gin frequently. They also engaged in other unsafe activities unexpected of juveniles.

Debisi's parents tried all they could to get him to see reason, but the boy felt they were unnecessarily intruding into his life.

"I don't really care about what you people think. This is the only time I could enjoy my youthful years," Debisi would reprove his parents. "This is not the 1950s; we're in the 1970s, for God's sake." Nobody seemed to be able to get across to Debisi, the formerly respectful boy that everyone loved.

Predictably, Debisi started engaging in further disparaging lifestyles. The rumor was everywhere that he smoked marijuana, and that looked scary to the other students. That was because the consumption of illegal substances was strongly frowned at by the general population. Everyone knew that Debisi was on the path to destruction because he lacked discipline.

Debisi, the erstwhile fast runner, started lagging behind the other athletes on the tracks. He could no longer keep up with their pace, although they used to run behind him in the past. Debisi withdrew from running shortly because marijuana and sports had nothing in common. One could either choose smoking or sports.

It was clear that Debisi was losing control, but nobody envisaged what happened next. The good-looking, brilliant, and agile boy started acting strange. He would say things that had nothing to do with what was being discussed. Debisi would also touch people inappropriately and laughed about it all. He frequently talked and giggled by himself, to other people's astonishment. People said marijuana had affected Debisi's brain.

Debisi's family did all they could to restore him to no avail. They took him to the mental health hospital, but the addicted boy snuck out frequently to smoke marijuana. He escaped from the facility eventually and started roaming the streets. Debisi was talking and laughing by himself the last night I saw him passing our street. He sounded very wild and far from the rest of the world.

Abiose was his father's first male child. He had sisters, but his father wanted a boy who would transfer the family's last name to the coming generations. Abiose's father was very pleased when the boy was born. He celebrated the new baby's arrival elaborately. The father was happier when guests told him that his new son looked just like him.

No one was surprised that Abiose's father spoiled him in many ways. The young boy had the latest toys. He wore up-to-date garments and shoes. His father rarely reproved him, but the man reprimanded Abiose's sisters for the same amounts of wrongdoing. All of these combined to make Abiose the spoiled child in the family.

Abiose grew up rapidly. He had access to many things that his peers lacked. He did not know much about being careful and frugal. He was lavish and wasteful. Abiose had many friends because he had a lot of freebies to give to them. Additionally, the boy lacked discipline. He thought he could get away with anything, because he was not used to being scolded.

No night party was considered successful without Abiose. The fun-loving, trendy boy started attending social engagements early in his life. He started smoking cigarettes and drinking alcohol shortly. He had money to buy the substances he should not be consuming as a minor. Expectedly, like-minded fun-loving youngsters flocked to him.

Abiose had all he needed to be successful in life, but indiscipline tried to rob him of good life. He could fly on the wings of his loving, caring, but over-generous father, who gave him more than he needed. Unfortunately, Abiose almost did not take advantage of what he had. He sailed through elementary school but struggled academically in the high school.

Lack of discipline, over-pampering, and a gang of pleasure-seeking friends almost robbed Abiose of good education. Hang-overs from partying prevented him from going to school sometimes. He struggled to pass the classes he should have passed in flying colors. He wobbled between success and failure without finding his bearings quickly.

Abiose managed to secure admission to college, but he continued to struggle. He joined several pleasure-based sororities on campus. He had money to throw around, and dated several girlfriends at the same time. Everyone seemed to know Abiose on campus because he did not graduate with his classmates. He did not pass all of the required courses a couple of years after his mates graduated.

It took a combination of misfortunes for Abiose to get his act together. His father died suddenly, and the university was about to terminate his lackluster years on campus. The money was no longer flowing, as Abiose's father left more debts than inheritance. Perhaps, Abiose needed the under-the-weather developments to turn his life round.

The erstwhile unruly, careless, and lavish young man discovered that he had two choices before him. He could either turn his life around or tumble down the hill of impishness. He chose the former. For the first time in his life, Abiose thought about life seriously. He understood that he was the only one who could build a positive future for himself.

Abiose accepted the challenges posed by his father's demise and the university's displeasure with his academic performance. He quit his usual flippant behaviors, dropped his fair-weather friends, and started working hard. He started doing his academic work and making the right choices.

Surprisingly, Abiose pulled himself out of the abyss of failure, but he could not make up for the time he lost. His old classmates were years ahead of him. A few of them became lecturers on the same campus, and many were already climbing on their jobs in the public and private sectors.

Abiose was grateful that he turned away from the wrong path before it was too late.

Abiose was able to salvage his life because he turned a new leaf before it was too late. He wasted a lot of time earlier, but he had hope after changing his ways. The day a carefree person turns his life around is the beginning of his journey to success. It is never too late for those who have turned their backs on the slapdash lifestyle to focus.

Fun'yo, Debisi, and Abiose were not alone. Many promising youths found themselves in those youths' shoes. They took the wrong turns and ended up on the flawed paths, because of lack of discipline. Many youths ended badly because they could not manage success.

It takes discipline to be successful in life. Living a productive life requires restraint. Discipline is about adhering to positive behaviors, having responsible sense of worth, and holding one accountable. It is about remaining oneself, instead of running wild with the crowd. Something is not right simply because everyone does it.

Once upon a time, long before the tortoise stopped being sneaky and manipulative, an acute drought traversed the animal kingdom and led to a severe famine. All animals felt the impact of the food shortage except the birds. All land animals tried to look for what to eat any way they could. The tortoise was not an exception, as he looked for ways to survive, too.

The tortoise was aware that the birds had something to eat. They soared high into the sky for the birds' festivals where food was very plentiful. The tortoise wanted to join the birds, but he had no feathers to fly.

"How can I fly to the sky with the birds?" the tortoise asked himself thoughtfully. "Perhaps I can borrow some feathers from the birds, and fly with them to the sky...But the birds don't like me."

All animals knew that the tortoise lacked discipline. He was selfish, rude, and pushy. That compelled everyone to think twice before befriending him. The tortoise realized that he would have a hard time borrowing feathers from the birds. All the same, he refused to give up. He planned to engage his persuasive and manipulative powers to get his wish from the birds.

"I'm aware that many of you don't like me, but I have nothing against any of you. As a matter of fact, I like each of you," the tortoise said at the sandy plot of land where the birds met near his neighborhood.

The birds were suspicious of the tortoise, but were amused by his enticing words. They knew how brash and inconsiderate the tortoise was. Everyone was impressed that the selfish and arrogant animal could make this gentle and respectful speech at the birds' gathering.

The Hidden Treasures in Gray Hair

"All living beings should be protective of one another. We are united by the fact that we all have life. None of us should be hungry when some know how to get food during a grim famine like this," the tortoise appealed to the birds' consciences.

Some of the birds agreed with the tortoise, but the majority of them were suspicious of his sweet tongue. The soft-minded birds pleaded with the rest, to please, hear the tortoise out.

Eventually, the tortoise came clean with the reason why he spoke nicely to the birds. "I came to borrow a feather from each of you, so I could fly to the sky with you. My family needs food, otherwise, we won't survive for another week."

Understandably, the birds were not convinced that they should lend their feathers to the tortoise. However, the crafty animal succeeded in convincing them in due course. The birds decided to lend the tortoise a feather each. The latter went home with a bag full of different feathers.

The tortoise wove the borrowed feathers together and his wife helped to glue them to his back. He looked beautiful more than the birds in the animal kingdom because of the colorful plumage from the diverse birds. The tortoise was ready to join the birds during their flight to the feast in the sky.

All the birds took to the sky on the appointed day, and the tortoise was not left behind. He joined the birds in the flight to gorge himself in the clouds. The tortoise was very happy that he could fly. He knew he could eat to the fullest, and even bring food down to the rest of his family. He praised his ability to convince the birds to lend him their feathers.

The tortoise succeeded in transforming himself so much that none of the birds recognized him. They all wondered who the colorful bird was, because they had never seen such multihued bird before. Some of the birds asked the new bird to tell them his name.

"My name is '*All of you*,'" the tortoise introduced himself to the birds as they flew to the sky. Later events revealed that the tortoise had a good reason for choosing that name.

All of the birds arrived at the sky without any incident. They were all pleased that they would start the bird festival and feasting shortly. All of them seated and waited patiently for the celebration to begin. The tortoise could not wait for the festivity to begin.

Shortly, the hosting sky-spirits laid a buffet of foods and drinks before the visiting birds. They brought more and more food till the table could no longer hold more. It was time for the bird to feast.

"Who has all of the food on the table?" asked the shifty tortoise unceremoniously.

"They belong to *all of you*," said the head waiter. "Enjoy!" he added and walked away.

"Everyone heard the head waiter; the food belongs to me. Remember, my name is '*All of*

The Hidden Treasures in Gray Hair

you,'" the tortoise said as he moved closer to the dishes. He grabbed the bowls one by one and ate as much as he could, without offering the other birds any of the food. He packed the remaining foods and drinks as "take-away" for his family. Nobody struggled with the tortoise because there was orderliness and respect back then.

The tortoise repeated the same gimmick when it was time for lunch and dinner on that day. The other birds were hungry beyond imagination. They were angry as well. They could not believe that one bird gorged himself while the others went to bed hungry.

As usual, the tortoise found it difficult to hide his lack of discipline. He thought he should reveal himself to the birds, and let them realize how unintelligent they were.

"I'm *Ijapa*, the tortoise you hated so much. You can see that I'm smarter than all of you after all," the tortoise bragged about his lack of sensitivity to the birds' plight. All of the birds wanted to get even with the selfish animal that borrowed their feathers and tricked them in the end.

The birds descended on the tortoise and demanded their feathers. They pulled the feathers from the ungrateful animal's back, and left him bare with his shell. The tortoise had no feathers left, but it was time for the party to fly back to the ground. The birds were pleased that they took their pounds of flesh from the tortoise.

The tortoise realized that he would not be able to fly back home with the birds. He begged them to reconsider their actions to no avail. Thereafter, the tortoise requested the birds to deliver a message to his wife when they land on the ground.

"Please, tell *Yannibo*, my wife, to lay all of the soft materials she could find outside our house later this evening." The tortoise sent a message to his wife. He planned to jump from the sky to the ground later in the evening when his wife would have prepared for his soft-landing.

The angry birds flew down to the ground, and decided to punish the tortoise. They told his wife that *Ijapa* wanted her to lay all the hard materials she could find in front of their house that evening. The tortoise's wife did as the birds told her. She looked for jagged metals, rocks, and hard woods, and laid them outside their house.

Ijapa looked down from the sky and saw his wife placing things in front of the house. Unfortunately, the tortoise was far away, and could not determine what she was laying outside the house. Regardless, the tortoise trusted that his wife was laying soft materials outside the house.

The tortoise prepared to plunge to the ground as the sun set. He was afraid that something bad might happen, but he had no option other than to jump. He had to return home to his family. He looked at the ground once again, and was pleased that his wife placed enough materials to

The Hidden Treasures in Gray Hair

break his fall. The tortoise dived to the ground in a free fall.

The undisciplined, greedy, pushy, and manipulative animal landed on hard materials in front of his house. His erstwhile smooth shell broke into many pieces. *Ijapa's* wife and children nursed his injuries for a long time before they healed. His wife managed to glue the broken shell together and placed it on *Ijapa's* back.

Regrettably, the tortoise's shell lost its smoothness, and has remained uneven till today. *Ijapa* disfigured himself permanently because of lack of discipline. The birds and the other animals were not amused by the tortoise's behavior. They could not understand why *Ijapa* was so covetous, impolite, and had no regard for accountability.

Chapter 11
ACCOUNTABILITY—
The Inevitable Remuneration

Generally, life is an equal opportunity place where those who sow sweet corn reap sweet corn and those who plant wild oat harvest wild oat. Men are answerable for their exploits, and women are accountable for their actions.

The only paved road that traversed the town meant little to me. I knew it came from somewhere and it meandered elsewhere, but I had no idea what those places looked like. The local people who had travelled through one or both directions of the road told many stories. However, I could only imagine what they were saying, being an elementary school pupil who had yet to travel out of the town.

Accordingly, it looked like I was going to burst with joy when Grandma said I would travel with her to *Iwaraja*. That was where my auntie's husband took her when she became ill. I was not sure if my happiness had to do with travelling out of the town for the first time, or because I was going to see my mother's sister who left home some weeks earlier.

I'm about to see the world! I exhaled with joy as I reflected over the significance of the development. I was about to venture out of town. I marveled at the news that we could even visit *Ilesha*, the larger town located some distance from *Iwaraja*. I could not wait for the scheduled travel date to arrive. The counting began instantly.

I used a piece of wood charcoal to mark the number of days on the wall, with one notch representing a day. I crossed out a notch every day. The days between when Grandma told me about the journey and the day we travelled seemed like the longest period of my life. A day appeared like a week, and a week like a month.

I'm travelling at last! I thought to myself as I hopped up Oga Banji's *korope*, the small lorry that transported people to other towns in the 1960s. I looked important as the neighborhood children came to say goodbye to me at the motor park. They said I would be more informed than them about the world when I returned from the journey.

Truly, the journey enriched my budding interest in how things worked. I started learning immediately the lorry sped toward the part of the road

The Hidden Treasures in Gray Hair

that was once unknown to me. I could not take my eyes off the trees and vegetations along the road as the vehicle passed them. The moving lorry appeared stationary, but the plants outside seemed to be rushing by. The latest development mesmerized me for a while, but I knew it was unreal.

"This is awesome!" I hummed to myself, as I sat beside Grandma. I tried to imagine how many unreal things looked real in life, like the seemingly motionless lorry and the "speeding plants." I knew that the vegetations were stationary, but the lorry was the one passing them.

My thought shifted briefly to the other experience that captivated me a few days earlier. I remembered seeing a *salamo*, the red ant, as I strode across a puddle of water on the ground. I stood and watched as the ant inched its way along the puddle, trying to go around. It could not step across the mini pond like I did.

Like a huge lake, a little puddle puzzles the tiny ants, but it remains a tiny pool of water to humans. The world is full of illusive issues! I kept thinking.

Many things appeared illusive to us children as we grew up. Some unreal things appeared real, and some real things appeared unreal. Fortunately, I was able to unknot some of the illusory things on my own. However, I depended on the reliable adults around me for unraveling the most arduous ones. The grown-ups were versed in finding answers to my questions.

The other young children and I simply dreamed about becoming successful in the future. Nevertheless, we seemed too young to understand what it took to be successful. We wished for achievements, daydreamed about accomplishments, and expected to be successful some day by chance, instead of through hard work.

"I'll become a great leader in the future," I often dreamed. "I'll promote peace around the world, fight for equality among peoples, and advocate social justice everywhere."

My grandparents supported my dreams, but understood that I needed more than daydreaming, wishes, and luck to achieve them. They untangled the illusive part of life by discussing accountability with me. They explained that those who did well in life would be rewarded, but those who did badly would get equal amount of consequences.

"What if someone doesn't succeed in life due to no fault of his? Will people still hold him or her accountable for other people's faults?" I asked my grandmother out of curiosity.

"The circumstances or the other people in someone's life may disrupt his or her accomplishment in life. But one cannot point accusing fingers at others or circumstances beyond certain points," my grandmother explained. "The reality is that people don't care about what the other people or circumstances did or didn't do when you were young. They hold you accountable for your life once you grow up."

"So, the child who lacked good parental upbringing cannot blame his parents for his or her failure?" I persisted, by rephrasing my previous question.

"Not for so long…People hold you accountable for your life once you become an adult," Grandma insisted. "Pointing accusing fingers doesn't work at that point. Three of the fingers on your hand point at you whenever you point an accusing finger at someone else," the elderly woman added philosophically.

Reflexively, I pointed my right hand's index finger at the door post, and marveled at the result. My grandmother was flawlessly right! Although my thumb and index finger pointed away from me, the middle, ring, and small (pinky) fingers pointed toward me. It was clear that whoever pointed an accusing finger at another person for his or her failure would have three of his or her fingers pointing at him or her. *Holding oneself accountable, instead of blaming others, cannot be farther from the truth*, I thought.

Grandma and Grandpa explained that nature had a way of repaying people back for what they did, and everyone got something back for his or her action. They insisted that people would get positive or negative responses for what they did, depending on their actions.

"Everyone will account for what he or she does in life. No one plants okra and harvests corn," Grandpa explained. "The consequences you get in life depend on the choices you make. What you do now would influence your future. You'll become prosperous if you work hard, but you'll become needy if you are indolent." My grandfather was a sharp shooter when it came to counseling young people. He told it as it was.

"Education is the modern choice that youths cannot avoid if they want to be successful. You'll go far in life if you get education. Those who determine the world's fate will befriend you if you gain knowledge," Grandpa persisted as he educated me about the magic of education.

"The shakers and movers of society will listen to you if you have education. Alternatively, you'll be stuck with your opinions if you lack edification, as many won't listen to what you have to say. I would have dined and wined with kings and queens if I had acquired educated. I was reduced to a local chief because I didn't have the education to carry me farther. I'm now accounting for my lack of modern education."

My grandfather did not even excuse himself for not having modern education. People could feel his passion and sense of loss when he spoke about education. He would have taken education seriously if he had been offered a second chance. Regrettably, he was aged and had a lot of responsibilities, too.

The Hidden Treasures in Gray Hair

"You have tried, Grandpa," I attempted to console my grandfather. "I think your lack of education had to do with the fact that most people in your generation didn't go to school. Back then, people saw farming as the profession for the real men," I added.

Clearly, Grandpa wanted his offspring to get education because of what he missed due to lack of education. Some of the young people in the family thought Grandpa overdramatized the role of education in the modern time. However, the man did not think he was saying enough.

"I've been a farmer for all of my adult life, but I've not gone beyond subsistence farming," my grandfather lamented.

I did not understand why Grandpa lamented being a farmer. Most people in the region described farming as a noble profession. They defined it as the regional vocation. The schools even had farms and celebrated the occupation. A popular song was composed for farming:

Farming is our land's vocation
Whoever fails to farm would steal
Education without hoe and cutlass
Is not complete; not complete

"Don't get me wrong," Grandpa explained where he stood on education and vocations. "One could pursue any profession—farming, teaching, carpentry, dressmaking, or home construction. One would only become better in his or her profession with education."

Grandma, who sat nearby, removing melons from their shells interjected. "The educated farmers enhance their farming with their education. The educated home builders know how to build the best structures, compared to the uneducated builders." I did not realize she was listening to our discussion till she spoke.

My grandfather's stand was very clear at that point. He simply wanted me to know that those who had education did better in their respective professions. I could not agree more with Grandpa, because nobody had anything to lose by enhancing his or her profession with modern education.

"Don't worry, Grandpa, I'll go to school and even go to the university," I promised the elderly man. "You don't lose everything if your offspring go to the university. We'll usher education into the family, and make sure it remains with the lineage for many generations to come."

Grandpa felt better each of the time I assured him that I would go to the university. The smiles on his face showed that he believed in me. He really wanted the youths in the family to break the vicious circle of illiteracy. I was willing to be one of those who will receive higher education in the family.

Grandpa and Grandma were right because the most successful people in the town had some forms of education. The local farmers were the hardest working people, but their successes and fame rarely went beyond the town. On the other hand, the educated folks were celebrated beyond the locality. They were known in the towns and villages in the region.

Grandpa was not alone in advocating education to the youths. Many elderly people in the town did the same. They lamented their inability to go far because of lack of education. It was clear that they wanted their offspring to go to school. Some of them did not mind paying so much for their children to get education.

I realized that my grandparents would not house, cloth, and feed me forever. I knew that I had to step in and care for myself at some points in life. It was clear that I would grow up to embrace a profession. I had no clue what the profession would look like at that point. Nonetheless, I did not want the profession that I would invest intensive labor into and get sketchy profit in return.

Grandma explained that all of the efforts that people put into what they did would add up, and account for what they get someday. She strongly believed that everyone was the designer of his or her fortune. My grandmother embraced the thought that those who succeeded worked for it, and those who failed got what they deserved.

It was not strange that I started thinking like my grandparents as time went by. I counseled my cousins who lived with their parents, and my friends in the neighborhood. I repeated all that my grandparents told me about accountability.

Some of the kids thought I was right, but some assumed that I was meddling with their lives.

I must concede that I was not a seraph. I had my own share of the childish impishness of that epoch. However, I did not take my eyes off of the light at the end of the tunnel. I focused on my desire to succeed, regardless of being a child when I was truly a child. I thought about my grandparents' counsels so often.

"Your tomorrow depends on the aggregate of the choices you make today. The days you go to school, arrive on time, pay attention to the teacher, and do your parts will add up," I told my peers. "On the other hand, the days you skip school, cut classes, disrespect the teachers, and act disruptively will add up, too. We all account for what we become in life."

Grandpa and Grandma went beyond education when talking about accountability. They characterized accountability as an encompassing phenomenon that included people's conduct. The elderly couple insisted that people needed good conduct to support their accomplishments.

The people addressed responsible individuals as "*Omoluwabi.*" That is, the one born with fine disposition. The person referred to as *Omoluwabi* must have good manners to earn that honor. He or she must be respectful, hardworking, trustworthy, generous, and believe in working for the common good of the people. Most people, young and old, aspired to be identified as *Omoluwabi*.

The Hidden Treasures in Gray Hair

Schools encouraged accountability, too. They admonished students to be courteous, hardworking, reliable, and kind to others, as everyone would account for his or her activities in the end. The elementary school, for instance, engaged folktales for encouraging accountability.

Once upon a time, there were two friends in a town. They were fond of one another and did everything together. The two friends couldn't do anything without consulting with one another. Everyone knew the two female friends in the town and its environs. The people used the two friends as the yardsticks for measuring real friendship.

"My dear friend, I need to tell you something," began the first friend. "I've been thinking of doing this for a while, but I thought I should tell you before I do it."

"What is it, my friend?" the second friend responded enthusiastically. "None of us has done anything without consulting with the other. Tell me, please. Who knows, I might be able to assist you with the plan."

The first friend was very happy that her friend showed interest in her idea even before she knew what it was all about. She was grateful that there was someone she could trust when it came to starting a new venture. As usual, she minced no words as she told her friend everything.

"Thank you, my good friend. I've been thinking of planting a cola tree, now that cola-nuts are very expensive. I guessed that I would earn some money from that venture."

"That's a very thoughtful venture," said the second friend. "I won't only support this idea, but I would help you to achieve it."

"You are my angel! What could I do without you, friend?" The first friend was elated that her friend liked her plan and even promised to support her.

The first friend did not expect her friend to discourage her from planting the cola tree. However, she was happy that her friend would take care of the tree with her.

The first friend got a cola-nut seedling and planted it a few days later. She watered the seedling on daily basis till it started budding. Then, she realized that she had to protect the cola from the domestic animals in the neighborhood. The goats and the sheep in the town were notorious for eating all of the foliages they had access to.

"My friend, I just realized that I needed a pitcher to protect the cola sprout from the animals," the first woman told her friend. "I think I need to buy the special pitcher for protecting young plants in the nursery," she added. When turned upside down, the pitcher protected the plant that grew through the hole in its middle.

"You don't have to waste your hard-earned money for buying a new pitcher when I have one that I don't use," advised the second friend.

The Hidden Treasures in Gray Hair

"How can I repay you back for the generosity?" The first friend showed her gratitude for the other woman's support. She was truly grateful that her friend was willing to give her a pitcher to protect the cola plant from the neighborhood animals.

The first friend accepted the pitcher and used it to protect her plant. The cola sprout started growing rapidly, and became a matured tree in no time. The first woman continued to take care of the tree till it started producing cola-nuts. Meanwhile, the pitcher remained around the tree.

"I can't believe that the cola tree started fruiting so soon," said the first woman. The nuts were very smooth and attractive. She harvested the first set of cola-nuts and gave them to her friend, for her earlier generosity.

"Thank you, my friend," responded the second woman. "You don't have to give me all of these cola-nuts; we are best friends after all," she added.

"You deserve it, my friend. I can't think of anyone who deserves it more than you." The first woman insisted that her friend deserved what she offered her.

The second woman accepted the cola-nuts eventually. The two friends continued their friendship without any problems. However, things changed when the first woman started selling her cola-nuts. People desired her cola-nuts, and she made a lot of money from selling them. She even sold cola-nuts to the merchants from neighboring towns.

The second woman became jealous because her friend was making a lot of money from cola-nuts. She started resenting her friend and making meanings out of every harmless thing she said. The jealous woman thought about how she could make her friend lose the cola tree.

"Yes! I have an idea," said the second woman underneath her breath. "I'm going to ask my friend to return my pitcher. She has to cut down the cola tree if she has to return the pitcher to me without breaking it."

Unknown to the first woman, her friend was about to ruin her fortune, by demanding for the pitcher. The first woman continued to make money by selling cola-nuts. She was a very generous woman, as she gave a substantial part of her profit to charity. Everyone in the town, including the chief, noticed her kindness.

"I'm sorry, my friend, but I have to take my pitcher back from you. I need to plant my own cola tree, too," the second woman said without expressing any guilt.

"You can't do that to me. You realize that I cannot remove the pitcher unless I cut down the tree. Please, allow me to buy you another pitcher," the first woman pleaded with her friend.

"I don't want another pitcher. I want the exact pitcher I gave you; the one around your cola-nut tree," the second woman insisted.

The Hidden Treasures in Gray Hair

The two friends talked back and forth about the pitcher till their neighbors became involved. They advised them to take the case to the village chief. Everyone was outraged that the jealous woman wanted her friend to cut down her cola tree. The people believed that the town's chief would not grant the mean woman's request.

The friends took the case to the chief eventually. The chief requested them to state their cases, and they did. The town's chief offered to give the jealous woman a new pitcher, in return for the one she gave to her friend. Regretfully, the envious woman insisted that her friend should return the exact pitcher she gave to her.

"I can't have something else; I want the exact pitcher I gave to her." The covetous woman repeated, as the chief appealed to her one more time.

"I can't stop you from having your wish, but remember that you'll account for your action someday. Accountability is an unavoidable phenomenon," the chief counseled the resentful woman.

The chief was surprised that anyone could be callous like the jealous woman. However, he had no option than to follow the town's decree. The chief understood that the owner of a property had the right to give or retrieve it as he or she wanted. The chief told the woman that she could take her pitcher back.

Nobody was happy except the invidious woman, who took joy in ruining her friend's fortune. She went home rejoicing that her friend would lose her cola tree. She watched her friend cut down the cola tree and returned the old pitcher.

The woman who lost her cola tree was sad, but the people helped her to get through the hard times. Some gave her money and other things to offset the income she lost due to losing her cola tree. The people remembered the good woman's generosity and positive attitude.

The good woman put the hard feelings behind her and moved on. She did not stop associating with her friend, regardless of the latter's ill behavior. She believed in the aphorism that everyone would harvest what he or she sowed at the apportioned time.

The two friends continued their relationships as it was before the pitcher incident. They exchanged visits as usual, and went to places together. Life returned to normal as the two friends lived as if nothing had happened to them. Their neighbors were surprised that the two women carried on with their friendship.

Time passed by quickly without further ill experiences between the two friends. The jealous woman soon gave birth to a baby girl. Everyone, including her friend, was very happy for the gift of a new baby. As usual, people presented gifts to the infant. The good woman bought a beautiful necklace for her friend's baby.

The jealous woman was surprised that her friend bought the expensive necklace for her new

The Hidden Treasures in Gray Hair

baby, in spite of how she had treated her. She thanked her friend and placed the necklace on her baby's neck. The jewelry looked nice on the baby, and everyone liked it.

The child grew up rapidly and started playing around the neighborhood, like the other children of her age. The young girl continued to wear the beautiful necklace presented to her by her mother's friend. However, it could not be removed from her neck since she had grown.

The people of the town wanted justice for the woman who lost her cola tree, because of her friend's covetousness. They pressured her to ask for the jewelry she bought for her friend's daughter. Everyone was willing to see the bad woman get paid for her bad behavior.

"Whoever takes back her pitcher should be willing to return someone's necklace," said an elder.

The good woman knew she couldn't get her necklace back, unless the girl's neck was severed off her body. She was not willing to see that happen, but she wanted her friend to learn something from her old mistake. She pretended that she agreed with what the people suggested.

"My dear friend, I must tell you something," the good woman whispered to her friend. "I didn't intent to do this, but I have to take back the necklace I presented to your daughter when she was a baby."

"Are you kidding me? My daughter is now grown. You cannot have your necklace back unless they cut my child's neck off her body."

The two women talked back and forth till their neighbors referred the case to the town's chief. As usual, the chief listened to both parties. He recalled that he had begged the jealous woman to no avail when she asked her friend to return her pitcher some years earlier.

"You know the rule. You have to return your friend's necklace. Our ancestors decreed that whoever owned a property had the right to give or retrieve it as he or she pleased," the town's chief judged.

The jealous woman's daughter was brought forward, and the town's executioner was about to do the unthinkable. Then, the good woman stepped forward and demonstrated the most courageous act of magnanimity in the town. She pleaded for mercy for her friend's daughter.

"I appreciate the people's gesture that everyone should account for his or her actions. However, we cannot punish the innocent child for her mother's unwarranted behavior. I want the child to keep the necklace," the good woman said to the chief and the people.

The chief and the people rewarded the good woman for her good manners. They gave her a farm full of cola trees. They fined the jealous woman a huge amount of money and shamed her in front of the whole town. Thenceforth, the good

The Hidden Treasures in Gray Hair

woman became a heroine figure in the town, but the jealous woman became an example of a bad friend.

Everyone will account for his or her deeds. People will remember those who did well. They will also remember the evils done by the others. The two friends accounted for their actions. The people detested the jealous woman for her absurd behavior. They admired the good woman for persevering and giving her friend a second chance.

Chapter 12
PERSEVERANCE—
The Resolve to Win

An open but unfamiliar secret of life is that no one is hopeless. Everyone knows how to do something right. Whoever thinks he doesn't know how to do something is yet to discover himself, or hasn't tried enough.

I learned that nobody was useless as I grew up. I discovered there were no hopeless or disabled people. I discerned, by chance, the good side of the young man that I wrote off earlier. I saw the good side of an indolent and drunken member of my community. Then, it occurred to me that everyone had a good side.

Itu was a promising young man. He had the physic of someone bound for success. He was strong and skillful. He dropped out of the high school, but had the skill of a smart person. He was also a competent fighter. Many thought *Itu* would end up as a heavyweight wrestler or boxer. In fact, *Itu* means "feat" in Yoruba.

Regrettably, *Itu* had his shortcomings. He was an alcohol and drug abuser. Many could not stand where he stood, because he reeked of *ogogoro*, the local gin he drank so often. Additionally, *Itu* was a heavy marijuana smoker. He did not have many friends in the community, except those who embraced the same lifestyle as him.

I did all I could to avoid *Itu*. I had nothing to do with him, except responding "hello" occasionally whenever he greeted me. I was a college graduate, and thought I should not be seen with a self-destructing fellow like *Itu*. I avoided making eye contact with him even when he tried to speak with me. I was not happy with the fact that he had all he needed to become a successful person, but he blew it on his own.

Itu was a chauffeur. I had to go downtown urgently one day, and there was no other vehicle but *Itu's*. At last, circumstance forced me to sit in the vehicle driven by the young man I disliked. I made sure that *Itu* was not drunk before I entered the vehicle. I could not smell any of the inexcusable substances on him.

Something unusual happened thereafter that made me reconsider *Itu*. Sitting in the passenger seat afforded me an unobstructed view of the surroundings. Traffic was very slow that day. The ve-

The Hidden Treasures in Gray Hair

hicles went to a standstill at some points. We were at one of the journey's idle points when trouble started.

A newspaper vendor held his paper to my face at an intersection. He thought I would patronize him after reading the headlines. I was not thinking of newspapers at that point, but I glanced at the headlines when the vendor refused to leave. I looked away shortly, and expected the man to leave. I thought I was done with the vendor, but the aggressive salesman was not done with me.

"You have to buy the paper," the vendor said as he looked at me intently. He wanted me to buy a newspaper, regardless of whether I wanted it or not. I realized that the poor guy could have been standing at the street corner for a while without patronage. I could understand his forceful sales tactic. I was thinking of buying one newspaper when the vendor became rude again.

"Do you want free news?" he asked sarcastically.

I decided to avoid the vendor, hoping he would leave after a while. It was not unusual for vendors to display their papers in people's views when traffic slowed down. Not everyone who looked at those papers patronized the sellers. The vendor was looking for trouble, but I thought he met the wrong person. I was not ready to argue with him.

"Answer me, Mister," said the troublesome vendor. "You have to pay for the paper for looking at it."

I hoped that the road would be free at that moment, so the car could move, and avoid the upsetting newspaper seller. However, I was wrong. The traffic remained as it was, and no vehicle moved. As if the vendor's existence depended on the sale of a single newspaper, he requested for the paper's money again.

"Give me the money for the paper now," the vendor yelled as he shoved the newspaper through the car window. However, I thought I should not reward the bully by paying for the newspaper that I did not want. I decided to remain calm regardless of the vendor's unsolicited menace.

"I'm the offended party here. You displayed your newspaper in my face against my will, thereby obstructing my view in a public place. I think everyone has the right to a clear view along a public passage without unwanted obstruction by fellow road users," I explained like a legal practitioner.

The bothersome vendor would not listen to any of my pedagogic reasoning. He reached for my shirt's collar as the vehicle started moving slowly again. He continued to yell at me, hoping that I would pay him when I felt embarrassed by his rash behavior. However, I did not budge.

Suddenly, something unexpected happened. Help came from an unusual quarter. *Itu*, the young

The Hidden Treasures in Gray Hair

man that I once thought of as a never-do-well fellow, did something that interested me for the first time. The muscular six-foot-tall man, whom nobody would brush past without noticing, did something spectacular.

"Leave the gentleman alone. Don't make me come out of this vehicle," rumbled *Itu* with his deep bass voice.

Like an elephant that no animal encountered without noticing, *Itu* made an instant impression on the troublesome vendor. He made the statement as if he did not expect any physical, verbal, or bodily opposition from the vendor. Regardless of his shortcomings, *Itu* loved to be taken seriously when he spoke.

I wished that *Itu* would allow me to take care of the whole thing by myself. I knew that something dastardly could happen to the vendor if he did not take *Itu* seriously. I had witnessed *Itu* fighting, and it was not pretty at all. The young man knew how to fight rough, when he chose to.

Providentially, the newspaper vendor walked away quietly after glancing at *Itu's* scarred face. I could feel the unspoken applause of the other passengers in the vehicle. I was happy that the vendor walked away unhurt, because I had never liked or appreciated violence. *Itu*, the drunker, drug abuser, and relegated member of the community, just saved the day.

Maybe nobody is useless. Perhaps there should be redemption for the challenged mem-

bers of the community. Maybe people should look at the good sides of people sometimes, and not concentrate on the negative sides, I started thinking. Then, I decided to be nice to everyone, even when I would not choose them as my best friends. After all, a devalued member of the community just stopped a bully from having a field day.

For the first time, I had a long talk with *Itu* when I had the chance to speak with him alone. I was frank about the fact that he had a good side, regardless of the bad side he often showed to the people. I let him understand how smart he was, although he dropped out of school. I explained that Itu would be successful and respected by the people if he kept his good side, and toned down the bad side.

Surprisingly, Itu was not aware that he had a good side. He wondered if anyone really thought he had something good in him. Additionally, he considered himself a failure. He admitted that he tried to act responsibly sometimes, but found it difficult to focus. I encouraged the young man to rediscover himself, and try harder to focus on being good.

"Try, try, and try again till you get it right; and remember that no one is perfect. You cannot afford to give up on yourself. You must allow the people to see your good side often," I counseled.

I encouraged *Itu* to be optimistic, as no one was doomed to failure till he or she gave up. I thought that everyone knew how to do some-

The Hidden Treasures in Gray Hair

thing right. Additionally, I believed that those who thought they did not know how to do things right were yet to discover themselves or yet to try their best.

Imagine a never-do-well drug abuser becoming a hero in a community. *Itu* demonstrated that a person written off can become a champion, if he or she shows his or her good side. Thereafter, I agreed that every mortal had a purpose, and nature did not create anyone for no reason.

Like the moon that has its bright and dark side, every human has good and bad sides. How fellow humans judge someone depends on the side they see or they assume they see. People would likely consider you a good person if they see your good side often, and would judge you a bad person if they see your bad side frequently.

Do you give up sometimes, believing that you have no good side? Do you assume that you cannot do anything right? Think again. Everyone has something good about him or her, and everyone knows how to do something right. The reality is that some people assume they cannot be successful, because they are yet to discover themselves or have not tried hard enough.

Sometimes, there is a thin line between one's success and failure. It is possible that some people give up when they only need to try one more time. Some people dwell so much on their perceived failures and deny themselves the success they deserve if they could try just one more time.

"Nothing good comes easy," goes a motivational saying. Giving up too soon is not a fine idea. Every good thing is achievable only when people try hard. Every great and noble idea often comes with a chain of frustrations. It is only the daring and tenacious person who takes home the prize.

Perhaps no one explained the concept of perseverance to kids better than Mr. Olatimilehin. Fondly called S.O. (Samuel Olaiya) by friends and admirers, Mr. Olatimilehin was my father's best friend. He was the most munificent and down-to-earth person I knew. He was charitable and approachable to a fault.

Hailed as *Ola-Ola* by others, Mr. Olatimilehin welcomed and tried all he could to help young people understand life better. As a school teacher, and later a high school principal, Mr. Olatimilehin helped students to understand the importance of not giving up.

I was in Mr. Olatimilehin's office one mid-morning as he addressed a downcast youth. The young man in discourse was going to quit school on the grounds that learning was difficult. He felt he would be happier by walking away from school and going home to do nothing in particular.

"You cannot walk away from school without trying harder," began Mr. Olatimilehin.

"I tried, but it was very hard. I'm fed up with learning. I don't want to learn again," the discour-

The Hidden Treasures in Gray Hair

aged boy replied, as if he had reached the end of tolerance.

"I believe you have tried, but you have to try harder," counseled Mr. Olatimilehin. "You have to keep on trying. The only one who stops learning is the dead. I'm a school principal, but I'm still learning."

"You don't have to learn again; you are the school principal." The discouraged boy tried to stop Mr. Olatimilehin from encouraging him further.

"I have learned a lot, but I'll keep learning, because no one knows enough till he or she dies. You still have to learn something, even if you choose not to go to school again." The older man kept prodding the young man not to give up.

"I want to drop out of school and learn some vocation," the youth said submissively.

"I understand your point," continued Mr. Olatimilehin. "The reality is that you are not a failure when it comes to academics. You only need to put in more efforts."

"What difference does putting more efforts in education make if I learn a vocation? I don't know what I want to do yet, but I know that I'm fed up with education." The boy was now sounding so frustrated, like someone at the end of his wits.

"The difference is that education enhances all vocations. Having some education does not remove anything from a vocation; it only augments it. I'm sure that you'll pass the remaining subjects if you put more efforts." Mr. Olatimilehin refused to give up on the anxious boy.

The educator in Mr. Olatimilehin kicked in as he tried to convince the disillusioned student. I never witnessed the bighearted man giving up on any youth. That was exactly what he was doing that mid-morning. I remained stationary, listening to the conversation. I found every bit of it useful—not only to the intended listener, but to all youth.

"You cannot give up on yourself" continued the principal. "I have the feeling that you'll be alright if you don't give up. Complete the high school before moving on. Then, you'll be useful to yourself, family, community, nation, or even the world."

The boy looked at Mr. Olatimilehin trustingly, as if that was all he needed someone to tell him. He motioned his shoulders submissively, and gestured his surrender with one hand on top of the other. For the first time, it appeared like the counseling was making a difference.

"Maybe I should try harder," the boy said. Then he started thanking the tenacious principal profusely for not giving up on him.

On a lighter mood, Mr. Olatimilehin encouraged the young man further. He no longer directed his words to him alone, but to the two of us who were with him in the office. I knew that Mr. Olatimilehin wanted me to benefit from what he had to say next.

The Hidden Treasures in Gray Hair

"Coincidentally, I just read something about the great inventors," enthused the principal. "The world now enjoys many conveniences because the inventors did not give up, in spite of the near misses and frustrations they encountered."

It appeared like someone automatically switched on a light in my head at the mention of the inventors. I had a lot of interest in how things worked and those who made them. That was another opportunity for me to learn about those who invented things that made the world comfortable.

"The planet would have remained in darkness if the pioneers of electricity had given up," the principal stated. "Thomas Edison and Joseph Swan did not give up either. They confronted a lot of disappointments, but they accomplished their objective of bequeathing the light bulb to the world."

"Please, tell us more about that," I said, my mind racing as Mr. Olatimilehin spoke. I was never bored when listening to the motivational speakers who knew what they were talking about. Such talks were even more interesting when the speakers went global.

"The Wright brothers, who pioneered the airplane, did not give up. Now, one can travel from coast to coast within hours, on an airplane. It is the same thing with the man who invented the telephone...I think his name was Graham Bell. People now speak with people across the ocean because he did not give up." Mr. Olatimilehin encouraged the two of us who were listening to him.

The school principal, educator extraordinaire, and the most amicable man of his time was still talking when the assistant principal walked into the office. Politely, Mr. Olatimilehin acknowledged his assistance's presence, and concluded his counsel on perseverance.

"Things may look bad, but they would start changing for good the day you start making them right. It is those who keep running when others stop who cross the victorious line. You have to keep trying." The principal said and dismissed the now convinced student.

The adults told different folktales to illustrate perseverance. One was about an orphan who refused to give up. The young boy lost his parents at a tender age. He had nobody left to look after him, because the other members of his family saw him as a burden. They rejected him one by one. Consequently, the boy took up the role of looking after himself at a very young age.

"The world has turned its back on me," the poor but very smart boy lamented. "The person I intended to lean on has thorns in his hands. The individual I begged to blow the dust off my eyes filled his mouth with hot pepper."

The poor orphan learned hard work early in his life. He worked for different grown-ups, so he could fend for himself. Fatefully, the adults took advantage of him. They defaulted in paying what they owed him. More than ever, life became very frustrating, but the boy did not give up. He kept trying without losing hope.

It appeared like the orphan was at the end of his wits at some points, but he resolved to keep on trying. He considered leaving the village when it appeared nobody cared about him anymore. He knew he should help himself now that he was fast becoming a man. He decided to relocate to a faraway village where he could start over again. The boy was willing to give himself another chance elsewhere.

The orphan packed enough provisions for his journey. He had a jar of honey, a sack of corn, a parcel of meat, and a gourd of water. He set out on his journey one fateful morning. He trekked alone on the dusty road that led to far away villages and traditions.

The orphan, who was determined to succeed no matter what, was full of hope. He kept himself busy by humming the folk songs sung by his parents when they were alive. He trekked the whole day and slept by a tree trunk along the road at night. He was afraid of the wild animals, but his determination to get away overwhelmed him.

"Could you please spare me some honey?" An anxious bee woke the boy up the following morning. The bee wanted the orphan to share some of his provisions. That was the age when insects, birds, and the other animals reasoned and spoke like humans. The boy had a good reason to say no. He had no other source of replenishing his provisions till he arrived at a village. However, he was not used to saying no.

"Oh, I will give you some of my honey," the boy responded. He did exactly what he said. The orphan moved on thereafter.

The boy kept walking till about midday when he became hungry. He sat in the shade of a mahogany tree and ate some corn. All the while the poor boy was thinking of the day he would overcome poverty. He was very sure that he would triumph someday. All of the teachings about perseverance by his parents were paying off.

"Would you be kind enough to give me some corn?" A bird approached the boy and asked for some food.

"I would give you some of my corn," responded the kind orphan. He was not only determined to survive. The boy also wanted others to survive. Perseverance was his watchword. The orphan sat up and opened the sack of corn. He gave the hungry bird a handful of corn. The bird thanked the boy profusely.

The boy started moving as the bird waved at him with gratitude. He kept going till the sun moved toward the western horizon. The boy was just settling down for dinner when a famished hyena appeared. The animal was clearly hungry and needed something to eat urgently. Else, he would

The Hidden Treasures in Gray Hair

not make it. As expected, the hyena pleaded with the boy to give him some food.

"Would you, please, spare me the bones from the meat you are eating?" The hyena asked.

"Of course, I would give you the bones. People eat meat and throw away the bones, after all," the boy responded candidly. Then, he offered the animal some meat with the bones. The hyena was so grateful to the generous boy. He moaned thanks to him endlessly.

The orphan was on his way the following morning. He walked quietly for hours till he became thirsty. He was just lifting the gourd of water for a drink when a crocodile approached and asked for help. The boy realized that the animal wanted something to drink so badly.

"Could you share your water with me, please? I'm so thirsty. I decided to take a walk from my home by the river, and I became disoriented," the parched animal implored.

"Sure, why not?" The orphan did not say no, even when he had a good reason to say so. He lifted the gourd of water and gave the crocodile a drink.

"I won't give up my desire to succeed," the orphan said as he continued his journey without letting up. He kept moving till he saw a village ahead of him. The orphan was glad that he was about to start his life anew again. He smiled quietly as he approached the huts ahead of him.

The orphan was moving to the middle of the village when he saw a crowd. He asked one of the villagers why a crowd had gathered at that time of the day. The villager explained that young men competed every time the village chief wanted to give away a daughter in marriage.

"The village chief gives a daughter, money, and other things to the young man who accomplishes the task he offers every year," explained the villager.

The orphan was delighted to hear the explanation. He thought that could be the break he had been waiting for. He reminded himself that he had never given up, regardless of the challenges he faced. The boy did not think twice before opting to try his luck.

"Does it matter if the competing young man is from another land and clime?" the orphan asked the villager.

"It doesn't matter, as long as you are competent and willing to face off with the other young men," explained the villager.

The tenacious orphan raised his hand quickly, and the village chief obliged him to join the group of aspiring young men. Nobody expected the dusty and gaunt-looking boy to win anyway. They assumed that he would only swell the crowd of those aspiring for the princess, the scarcest commodity in the village.

The Hidden Treasures in Gray Hair

"Whoever identifies my daughter among the pack of beautiful ladies will marry her," the village chief gave the young men their task for that year.

The competing young men became disillusioned instantly, because none of them could identify the chief's daughter. The village custom dictated that the princesses be raised in other villages. They only returned when they were old enough to get married.

Some of the aspiring young men withdrew from the competition immediately. They thought it was more respectable to withdraw than get eliminated disgracefully. The orphan was surprised like the other young men, but he was not discouraged. He thought he had nothing to lose, after all. He prepared to take another risk in his desire to succeed.

Just then, a bee buzzed on the orphan's ear. The boy attempted to brush the upsetting insect away with his hand. However, the bee spoke into the boy's ear.

"I'm the bee you gave some honey on your way to this village. It is my turn to repay you for being kind to me," the bee explained. The insect offered to fly ahead of the boy and land on the chief's daughter.

The bee did exactly what he promised the orphan. He landed on the chief's beautiful daughter, and flew away without anyone noticing what happened. The boy stepped forward and lifted the chief's daughter's hand, to the amazement of her father. The chief was astounded, but he was not pleased that it was the poor, scrawny orphan who pointed his daughter out.

"You won the contest, young man; but you cannot have my daughter so fast," the aggrieved chief said to the orphan.

The village chief usually gave one task to the competing young men every year. However, he decided to change the rule at the end of the game, because he did not want the poor young man to marry his daughter. He decided to give a tougher task to the orphan. He thought he would not get it right this time.

"You have a day to separate the mixed mount of corn, millet, and sorghum into separate stacks. Then, you can have my daughter if you deliver," the village chief advised the orphan. Anyone would have been discouraged at that point, but the young man in question never gave up. He agreed to accomplish the new task.

A moment later, the bird that the boy fed on his way to the village appeared and offered to help him. The bird told the orphan not to worry, as he would go back home and invite other birds to accomplish the new chore.

"What if the king's servants see you? They could hurt you, or something." The orphan worried that something bad could happen to the bird.

"Don't worry, my friend. The tiger can only watch the bird in the air; it cannot fly up into the sky to catch it for dinner. The king and his servants

The Hidden Treasures in Gray Hair

cannot reach us." The bird advised the orphan to have faith in him.

True to his word, the bird returned with a cloud of birds. The birds were experts in separating grains.

To the bewilderment of the village chief and onlookers, there were three hill-sized stacks of corn, millet, and sorghum as they inspected the task later that evening. The chief was confused, but he realized that it was about time to release his daughter to the poor young man he so despised.

"Alright, you won again. But, you have to eat a cow, including the bones, by yourself before you could have my daughter," the village chief yelled.

The orphan was left in a room with stacks of cow meat and bones to consume all by himself. Something happened as the young man settled down to eat the meat. The hyena he fed along the way showed up with the other members of his family. They entered through the hole they made in the wall. The animals ate all of the cow meat and bones within a short period of time, to the boy's applause. Then, the animals exited and blocked the hole in the wall.

The village chief did not applaud like the orphan did moments earlier. He was sad when he came to inspect the cow meat and bones. He was shocked that they were all gone. All that the chief needed to do was to hand over his daughter to the most tenacious contestant he had ever accosted. The chief knew that the game was up.

Regretfully, the village chief would not let go his daughter any sooner. He had one more onerous task for the poor orphan. He was sure that the young man would not complete the task, as no one had accomplished it in the whole kingdom.

"Here's your last task, young man. You have to swim across the *Danger River* and bring me a sack of apricot fruits on the other side." The village chief ordered. The river was so named because it was full of ruthless crocodiles. The chief could not backslide if the orphan accomplished the task this time.

"You've succeeded this far, but you can't go any further. The child who has more clothes than the adult cannot boast of having more retired clothes than the adult. After all, the adult had been using and retiring clothes before the child was born. Your tricks cannot surpass mine," the chief bragged about the young man's perceived failure. He was sure that the orphan would fail the last task.

Everyone was weary of the chief's antics, and wanted it to end. "The curse has now surpassed the stolen item. The chief's needle got stolen, and he invoked the thunder to strike whoever stole it," a village elder complained about the chief's tough tactics.

The orphan worried as he stood at the riverbank. He looked at the somber faces of the on-

The Hidden Treasures in Gray Hair

lookers, and felt sorry that they felt that way. Regardless of his feeling, the young man would not give up at that point. He was determined to be successful after all of the hard times he had been through. The resolute orphan jumped into the dangerous river.

"Don't be scared; I'm here to help, my generous friend." That was the crocodile the orphan shared his water with on the way to that village. "Sit on my back and allow me to carry you to and from the riverbanks. All of the crocodiles in the river will grant you safe passage at my request."

The onlookers were surprised as the crocodiles lined both sides of the crocodile that carried the orphan. The people could not contain their astonishment and joy as they cheered vigorously. It amazed them that the once dangerous animals were not only harmless this time, but one of them even carried the young man.

Triumphantly, the orphan traversed the *Danger River* unscathed. He returned with a sack of eye-catching apricot fruits for the village chief. The chief and the people witnessed the orphan as he crossed and returned across the river. Clearly, it was difficult for anyone to deny that he accomplished the task. Additionally, the apricot trees were only on the other side of *Danger River*. The orphan could not have found the fruits in the village.

Eventually, the chief gave his daughter to the orphan. The chief made the young man a subchief over half of the village. Additionally, the orphan received a quarter of the chief's wealth. The once-deprived boy became an affluent young man, because he persevered and remained courageous to the very end.

Chapter 13
COURAGE—The Attribute of the Valiant

The courageous person dares to do what others preach but don't do often. Many advocate the truth but cannot stand the truth. It is only the gallant who does the audacious things advocated by many, but done only by a few.

It was an era of avoidable rebellions in Nigeria. The palpable tension around the country was frightening. A civil war broke out in the wake of the protracted political, economic, and religious mistrust between the ethnic groups. Justifiably, the *Igbos* became outraged after a spate of persecution in a particular part of the country. They attempted to secede and form a new nation called *Biafra*.

The remaining ethnic groups were not best of friends, but they formed a common ground against the seceding *Igbos* anyway. Subsequently, the federal military fought *Biafra* soldiers to submission in the war of attrition fought between 1967 and 1970. Different accounts put the military and civilian casualties of the war between one and 1.5 million people.

As if the bad news was not enough, another uprising reared its head in my region as the civil war raged in the battle fields. The regional government was exploiting the *Yoruba* farmers through corrupt practices and threat of higher taxes. *Agbekoya*, the farmers' union, meaning "the farmers who repulse hardship," revolted against the plan to increase taxes on cocoa, the regional cash crop. The local revolt lasted from 1968 to 1969.

The people worried about many things. Nearly everyone knew someone in the military. *Oga Ayo "Ko-Large,"* our distant relative, was in the federal army. The prices of common goods were going up. The regional government was aggressive in its efforts to keep the farmers in check. The young children, who could not fathom the depth of the crisis, were the only ones who managed their fears about the whole development.

I was young, but I had reasonable knowledge of what the region and the nation were going through. I worried whenever the neighborhood farmers gathered at my grandfather's house. I was anxious that Grandpa would be arrested and I might never see him again. The whole town worried about the future, because no one knew what

The Hidden Treasures in Gray Hair

would happen next. To me, the whole development ended up as my first lesson in courage.

Grandpa was not rich, but he was a courageous peasant. People flocked to him for reassurance and advice as the tough times raged. I heard and learned a lot from my grandfather at that time, because I was very close to him. I learned something from what he told the people who sought his counsel. The house was rarely short of someone talking to my grandfather.

"No one knows what would come next. The whole society is taking a hit," *Baba Ajao*, an elderly man on our street, said as the elders sat in front of our house.

"Don't give up," my grandfather responded. "Keep running when the masquerader chases you. The masquerader gets tired just as you get tired. The hard times don't last forever; they wear out as the people wear out."

"Life is frustrating these days, with the regional government trying to over-tax our means of livelihood," lamented *Baba* James, who owned the house opposite ours. He was frustrated by the proposed hike in cocoa tax.

"You are not alone. The ant is frustrated by its small size, but the hippopotamus is frustrated by its giant size," my grandfather explained philosophically. "No one is comfortable with his condition at this time. Everyone is frustrated by something in the country."

"Everybody is affected one way or the other," added *Baba* Sao, who was visiting from *Odo'se*, a distant neighborhood in the town.

"That's true, *Sao*. The poor suffers, and the rich does not enjoy his wealth. The worm has no teeth, but the elephant has no lips to cover its giant teeth. No one has everything going for him right now." Grandpa remained philosophical as ever. I could not shift my gaze away from him as I listened to his mastery of rational aphorisms.

"I'm upset that the leaders' actions are affecting the people adversely. Didn't they think before they made the mistakes that led to the messes?" I added my childish contribution to the discussion.

My grandfather looked at me warmly, and nodded his head approvingly. He was my biggest indulger in knowledge-seeking. He encouraged me to participate in knowledgeable discussions with adults. I owed him much of the wise sayings I knew as a child. Grandpa emboldened me by talking about how smart he thought I was.

"You are right, my son, but we cannot allow the frustrations to deter us. Life's frustrations are everywhere. Everyone has one. Anger would not end the frustrations, but knowing that we are not alone would console us. Let's be courageous more than ever."

My grandfather was right. Courage carried the people through the hard times. Everyone demonstrated bravery in some ways. The ordinary person worked harder to keep the tough times at bay. The federal and *Biafra* soldiers fought gallantly to defend what they believed in. The *Yoruba* farmers stopped the regional government from taking advantage of them.

Perhaps the most memorable story of courage told by the local people about the civil war was about the "*Black Scorpion.*" Colonel Benjamin Adekunle, Commander of the Nigerian 3rd Marine Commando Division, nicknamed the Black Scorpion, was reputed to have used his potent "black magic" to suppress the *Biafra* soldiers when it was necessary.

With courage, everyone appeared to win in the end. Nigeria remained an indivisible nation at the end of the civil war. The nation breathed a sigh of relief when General Yakubu Gowon, the military head of state, declared Nigeria as a united people after the unfortunate civil war that lasted thirty months.

"To keep Nigeria one is a task that must be done...No victors; no vanquished," General Gowon declared about the unfortunate hostilities.

Courage is the ability to support what the sense of right and wrong dictates, and not what is in vogue or what the trend says. It is the capacity to turn away from the fashionable but contemptible course taken by many, and take the route chosen by conscience. Courage is the audacity to stare danger in the face in the course of doing what is right. Courageous deeds are not necessarily easy, well-liked, or out of harm's way.

Courage is also the aptitude to come clean and embrace humility when one errs or makes a mistake. Those who stick to their points when it is clear that they are wrong are not courageous. Although, courage means daring to win, it is also the acceptance of reality if one loses. Those who make getting their ways a matter of life and death are cowardly. Courageous people understand and accept when they give their best shots but run short of victory.

Perhaps courage is the most compelling attribute of life. It appears as the central column among the pillars of character. The other affirmative traits that set people apart in life hinge on courage. For instance, people need courage to succeed. Success is not achieved by those who lack the nerve to accomplish. Also, those who are short of courage hardly have solid character. They bend to the directions that trend and events blow them.

Discipline requires courage. Those who have no guts cannot stand by what is right. They are easily swayed by the men and women of easy virtue. It takes a man, woman, or child with courage to act responsibly. Otherwise, they would agree to what influential, but reckless, peers ask of them. It takes courage to be a good citizen in a world full of those who detest authorities.

The Hidden Treasures in Gray Hair

Those who are deficient in courage are hardly ethical. It is easier for them to go with the popular culture, instead of espousing decency. Humility, caring, trustworthiness, obedience, and fairness are the other attributes of the courageous. It is courageous people who dare to set themselves apart in life—not the wishy-washy people who are afraid to stand by decorum.

Life is a tricky ocean that one must swim across. It takes the courageous to whirl through the depths of existence. Life is not always a straight boulevard; it is sometimes a shady and eerie alley. Existence dispenses fortune the way it chooses. Life is less demanding for some, but lonely, cold, and hard-hitting for others. It is full of challenges, regardless of one's political, social, or economic status. It is the courageous who confronts the predicaments of life precisely.

The youths in my neighborhood and I engaged in some acts of courage at some points. We were underprivileged children who decided to make the best out of our conditions. We resolved to confront the vicious circles of life positively. We chose not to remain the victims of circumstances, but to take advantage of the bad situations. Other kids engaged in ridiculous activities and claimed boredom. Courageously, we got busy with manual labors, so we could earn some money.

We needed the money for a lot of things. Some needed money for clothes and shoes to celebrate the New Year. That was the time of the year when youth showed off their new clothes and shoes. The younger children needed money for soccer balls, toys, and games. Older children needed money for table-tennis boards and their accessories, and the other more expensive things. Some children needed money for the books and school supplies their parents could not afford. Others wanted money for school excursions.

I sometimes followed Oga Imisi (my uncle), Oga Femi (my uncle's friend), and Adeniran (my second cousin) to construction sites. Occasionally, we met other boys and girls from our neighborhood at some sites. David, Clement, Adejare, Dare, Kolade, Tuyi, Oluwasola, Feyi, and the other courageous youths participated in manual labors sometimes. Occasionally, we fetched water from nearby ponds for mixing gravel, sand, and cement. We moved blocks from a location and handed them to the bricklayers at other times.

Bricklaying was not the only manual labor we engaged in to earn money. We sometimes worked on the farm. Local farmers hired youths during the cocoa processing season. At other times, we would cut palm fronds and reeds from the swamp and weave baskets for sale. We usually sold the baskets to market women and housewives, who used them for different purposes. Some farmers' wives bought our baskets and used them at their farms.

I engaged in other money-making ventures, like hawking kerosene around the town. I would

The Hidden Treasures in Gray Hair

buy a gallon of kerosene and resell to people in small bottles. Many of the people needed kerosene for household lanterns and cooking stoves. Relatives and neighbors also requested me to sell cooked rice and stew for commissions. I was a gas station attendant for a while. The money I earned relieved my grandparents a bit, because I was able to pay for some of the things I needed on my own.

"I commend your courageous attitude to life. Hard work does not kill; it is laziness that kills." My grandmother praised and encouraged me to keep fighting as I fought poverty.

Additionally, Grandpa admonished me to say no to destructive lifestyles. He insisted that those who engaged in appalling behaviors because their peers did the same were not courageous. My grandfather advised me to create my own path when my peers took the wrong path. He thought that brave youth should stand on their own pedestals if their peers stood on the wrong platforms.

Thus, I tried to say no when I had to say so. I declined a friend's dire gift when I stopped over at his place during a long vacation. Spending time with friends was one of the ways we spent our holidays in those days. "Bliss" appeared trendier than me, because he associated more with the popular youths in the town. I called him Bliss because he appeared vivacious and hospitable most of the time.

Bliss was very hospitable when I stopped at his place that afternoon. He was concerned about what to offer me. The host usually felt obliged to offer the guest something to eat or drink, in line with *Yoruba* tradition. Reciprocally, the guest may not decline what the host offered. Thus, people sometimes felt pressured to eat or drink what they did not really want.

"I have something special for you," suggested Bliss. He pulled a small cellophane bag from under the bed. Something told me that the bag's content was not special after all. "I'm not sure if you smoke, but I should ask you anyway." He added, while smiling coyly. He probably anticipated that my response would be different from what he expected.

"Thanks, but I should say no. I don't smoke, and I didn't expect you to smoke either," I responded as I dashed toward the door. "It was nice to see you. Have a fine afternoon."

"Well, you can't stop me from doing this," I heard Bliss saying as I walked away. I left the place without looking back.

That was the last time I went to Bliss's house. I knew I should not associate with someone who embraced a destructive lifestyle. After all, my grandmother said the sheep that associated with dogs would eat what dogs ate. I was afraid that what happened to Debisi, who developed a mental problem after using illegal substances, could happen to Bliss.

The Hidden Treasures in Gray Hair

It takes courageous youths to say no when their friends ask them to engage in life-shorting behaviors. Many young people do not like certain behaviors. However, they engage in them simply because their friends ask them to do so. They are afraid of losing their friends' companionships. It does not occur to them that they could say no to wayward friends.

A reality of life is that one loses nothing by losing bad friends. Your friends are bad if they adhere to destructive behaviors when you tell them to stop. Good friends listen when one asks them to stop inexcusable behaviors. We live in a free world these days. One should not enslave himself or herself to disparaging behaviors because his or her friends do those things.

Courageous people are capable of dumping bad friends and moving on with good friends. It is painful to abandon the friendship that one has invested time, vigor, and efforts into. Nevertheless, the pain that one gets by remaining with bad friends does not worth it. Courageous people select their friends, but cowardly people allow bad people to select them as friends.

Many youths are good on their own, but they get into trouble because of the friends they keep. They are not courageous enough to say no when their friends ask them to participate in appalling behaviors. You may not break the law directly with your friends. However, you could share in their consequences if you are around them during arrest.

Once upon a time, there was a boy born during a major epidemic. The endemic ailment killed most of the children born at that period. However, the boy did not die. He fell sick like the other children, but he held on to life courageously.

The boy's parents nicknamed him "*Divine's Will*." The king of that town was not pleased with the name given to the growing child. He was jealous that his parents named him "*Divine's Will*" instead of "*King's Will*." The king believed that all of the people lived by his will, and not by the will of some unknown divine.

Thus, the king had his eyes on the innocent boy. He did a lot of things to frustrate him as he grew up. It was part of the custom for young people to work for the king from time to time. The king gave *Divine's Will* more work than the rest of the youths who came to work at the palace. Providentially, the boy was so courageous in spite of the frustrations from the king. He did everything he was asked to do without complaining.

Ordinarily, the boy's parents expected the king to be glad that *Divine's Will* was hard-working. Nevertheless, the king grew more resentful that the boy was so courageous. He was afraid that the people would force him to abdicate the throne and make the boy the king when he grew

The Hidden Treasures in Gray Hair

up. The town had the tradition of making the most courageous person the king. Thus, the king wished the boy could just drop dead. He could not stand another courageous man in the town.

Inadvertently, *Divine's Will* upset the king more as he grew up. He became a very handsome, hardworking, and clever young man. He was even more courageous than the other youths in the town. He was smarter than the princes and the princesses, too. That did not sit well with the king. Now, he wanted *Divine's Will* to die at all cost. The king conspired with his lead adviser to kill the young man.

"I know how we could kill *Divine's Will*," suggested the adviser. "Your Highness, you could ask him to complete an assignment. Then, we would sabotage his efforts and make him fail. Thereafter, we would put him to death for failing to accomplish the royal assignment."

"That was very thoughtful of you," replied the euphoric king.

The king invited *Divine's Will* and gave him a ring. He requested the young man to hold the jewelry for seven days, and return it thereafter. The king explained that the ring meant so much to him, but he allowed those he loved to hold it for days at a time. The king lied to *Divine's Will* that he deserved to wear the ring because he was courageous. Conclusively, the king urged the man to keep the ring very well to avoid punishment.

"Whoever fails to return the ring to me on the seventh day would be put to death," warned the spiteful king.

"Please, accept my gratitude, your Royal Highness," *Divine's Will* thanked the king and went home with the ring.

As a sincere husband, *Divine's Will* showed the ring to his wife. He advised that the king requested him to keep it for seven days and return it thereafter. He had no reason to keep the ring without telling his wife about it. He thought everything would be fine.

Thereafter, the king and his lead adviser invited *Divine's Will*'s wife. They gave her some money and requested her to steal the ring from her husband. The king advised that the woman should not allow her husband to know that she stole the ring.

"You must return the ring to me immediately after stealing it from your husband," the king commanded.

Divine's Will hid the ring under the bed, and hoped that he would retrieve and return it to the king in seven days' time. Then, he carried his net and jumped into his canoe for a fishing expedition, as he was a fisherman. He paddled his canoe and caught fish throughout the day before returning home to his family. As usual, his wife sold the fish in the market. *Divine's Will* continued to look forward to returning the king's ring on the seventh day, as agreed upon.

The Hidden Treasures in Gray Hair

Sadly, the ring was gone when *Divine's Will* looked for it under the bed. His wife had stolen and returned it to the king. The young man looked everywhere, but he could not find the prized ring. He lit a lamp and swept everywhere, but the jewelry was nowhere to be found. *Divine's Will* became distrust because he knew what the king would do if he could not find the ring.

"I'm in trouble," *Divine's Will* said to his wife. "The king would put me to death if I could not find his ring." The young fisherman lamented. His wife pretended as if she was looking for the ring with him, but she knew it was already with the king. *Divine's Will*'s wife pretended to be sad like her husband. She frowned and looked sad like him, too.

Unknown to *Divine's Will*, the king and his lead adviser had thrown the ring into the river. They were sure that the jewelry would sink into the bottom of the deep river, and nobody would be able to retrieve it. The two of them believed they were close to putting *Divine's Will* to death. Then, the king would no longer contend with another courageous man in the town.

Divine's Will became even more courageous. He was sad, but moved on without allowing the incident to grind his life to a halt. He decided to return to the river and catch a fish before the seventh day. *Divine's Will* wanted to eat a good fish meal before the king put him to death. The courageous young man wanted to die as a comfortable man.

The young fisherman went back to the river and cast his net inside for a fish. He labored for a long time without catching anything. However, *Divine's Will* did not give up. He remained courageous to the very end. He caught a fish just as the sun was setting along the western horizon. Then, he returned home with the only catch.

Divine's Will brought out a knife and began to prepare the fish. He cut the fish's guts, and something phenomenal happened. The king's ring popped out of the fish's bowel. The young fisherman could not believe his eyes. He invited his wife to come and see what happened. The woman was equally bowled over. She could not figure out what the king would do to her when her husband returned the ring to him.

Divine's Will's constant demonstration of courage paid off once again. He returned the king's ring to him. The king was astonished more than anyone else. Rather than be satisfied, he became irritated more than ever. He wanted to kill the courageous fisherman at all cost. The king invited his lead adviser, and they returned to the drawing board of shenanigans once again.

The king decided to send his lead adviser and *Divine's Will* to a nearby village. The village was the town's protectorate, and the people looked up to the king to send a new chief whenever their chief died. Coincidentally, the village chief died around that time, and they needed a new chief. The king wanted his lead adviser to become the

The Hidden Treasures in Gray Hair

new village chief. However, he wanted the adviser to execute *Divine's Will* thereafter.

Expectedly, the king sent a message that the villagers should install his lead adviser as the chief. He also mandated his adviser to kill *Divine's Will* as soon as they install the former as the village chief. Unknown to *Divine's Will*, the king was trying to kill him again. However, the brave fisherman continued his life undaunted. He was courageous enough to believe that the just would triumph in the end.

The king's lead adviser and *Divine's Will* left the town for the village shortly. The adviser expected that he would become the chief, and he would order *Divine's Will*'s death soon after his coronation. As courageous and humble as ever, *Divine's Will* offered to carry all of their supplies. Thus, the king's adviser walked without carrying any luggage.

The villagers were looking forward to receiving their new chief. Regrettably, they saw two men when they were expecting just one. They were confused, as they could not figure out which of the two men would become the chief. The king's adviser insisted that he was the one chosen by the king to become the village chief, but the villagers were not sure. They could have sent someone to the town to verify with the king, but they wanted to coronate a chief immediately.

The villagers decided to consult the oracle, to find out which of the two men should become the

Dele Ajaja

new chief. Fortunately for *Divine's Will*, the oracle advised the villagers to install "the humble one" as the chief. The villagers noticed that it was the humble and courageous *Divine's Will* who carried the men's supplies to the village.

Therefore, the villagers installed *Divine's Will* as their new chief. They were upset that the king's adviser lied to them, or so they thought. The villagers decided to put the king's lead adviser to death, instead of *Divine's Will*. In the end, the mischievous king's adviser died, but the courageous fisherman became a chief. His fortune of being a courageous and good citizen paid off.

Chapter 14
CITIZENSHIP—The Bequest of the Patriot

The ship returns to the harbor after sailing the sea. The parrot returns home after an exciting outing. People may reject you elsewhere, but home will always welcome you back.

Grandpa made some money during a cocoa season, and applied for a *rediffusion* box. *Rediffusion* was the brand name of the London-based company that distributed the single-channel radio box. The *rediffusion* was an isosceles-trapezoid shaped box, with the longer side on top and the shorter side in the bottom. The box had a round speaker in the middle, and an on-off volume knob below. The *rediffusion* played music, broadcast news, and the other government-approved programs in the old Western Region of Nigeria.

Dele Ajaja

The *rediffusion's* single cable traversed the town on slim metal poles. *"Oga Rediffusion,"* the man in charge of the town's *rediffusion* office, connected the box inside the house to the *rediffusion* line outside with a piece of black wire. The *rediffusion* office relayed the signals from the regional capital from morning till night. The box was a delight to the neighborhood children, who often came to dance to the music of Hubert Ogunde, I.K. Dairo, Rex Lawson, Dan Maraya, E.T. Mensah, Bobby Benson, Haruna Ishola, James Brown, Elvis Presley, and Louis Armstrong.

    I had unrestrained access to Grandpa's *rediffusion* because I was his favorite grandson. I usually climbed a wooden bench to turn on or off the box in the corner where it hung upstairs. More neighborhood children jostled to be my friends, so they could listen to my grandfather's *rediffusion*. I was proud as the one that Grandpa sent upstairs in our two-story house to turn on or off the box. It was loud enough for people to hear downstairs.

    I was fully in control of the *rediffusion* whenever my grandparents went to the farm and allowed me to stay at home. The radio station played music a lot and aired the news a few times a day. Every news segment began with the memorable line expressed with *gagan*, the "talking drum:"

When Olubadan passes on,
Who becomes the chief?
When Olubadan passes on,
Who becomes the chief?

The Hidden Treasures in Gray Hair

When Olubadan passes on
Who becomes the chief?

Olubadan was the traditional ruler of Ibadan, the capital of erstwhile Western Region of Nigeria. Like the other foremost traditional rulers in the country, the Olubadan was well respected by the people. He was not just a royal father, but the king of the regional capital. Thus, the importance attached to his position by the regional broadcasting corporation.

In addition to listening to music, I paid attention to the other things broadcast by the *rediffusion*. It was a good source of current affairs. It commented on the Cold War between the U.S. and the U.S.S.R. The *rediffusion* paid a lot of attention to the historical unrest in the Middle East. It also mentioned Neil Armstrong of the U.S. as the first human to step on the moon, after arriving on the spacecraft, *Gemini*.

Additionally, the *rediffusion* was a good source of civic education. I learned a lot about the other ethnic groups in the country on the *rediffusion*. I heard the leaders talking on the box, too. The *rediffusion* often played the first stanza of the old Nigerian national anthem before the head of state addressed the people:

Nigeria, we hail thee,
Our own dear native land,
Though tribe and tongue may differ,
In brotherhood we stand,
Nigerians all, and proud to serve
Our sovereign Motherland.

The *rediffusion* discussed many topics, including citizenship. There were dialogues and jingles on the social contract between the people of the nation. Most of the discussions centered on how the citizens can make the country a better place. Some of the discussants urged the people to be patriotic by espousing transparency, accountability, and integrity. Others recommended that the people should help build a Nigeria devoid of corruption, nepotism, sectionalism, and religious bigotry.

Listening to the civic discussions on the *rediffusion* paid off shortly. Mrs. Olafunmiloye initiated a chat on citizenship one afternoon. I was glad that the elementary school teacher brought up the dialogue on citizenship, because I had been paying attention to my grandfather's *rediffusion*. The teacher described citizenship as having allegiance to one's country, doing one's part, and getting protection back from the country.

"The nation confers rights to the citizens and expects responsibilities back from the citizens. What are some of the ways the citizens could give something back to their country?" Mrs. Olafunmiloye asked. I raised my hand immediately, and the teacher pointed at me.

"The citizens could support the country by embracing transparency, accountability, and integrity," I responded confidently, almost quoting what I heard on Grandpa's *rediffusion*.

"That was very thoughtful of you, Ayodele," the teacher said gleefully. "The nation can only make progress when the citizens are transparent, accountable, and have integrity...Now, what are the other ways the citizens could support the country?"

I could not resist the temptation of showing what I learned from the *rediffusion*. I was glad that I had been paying attention to the *"box that talks without getting a response* back." The *rediffusion* was so tagged because people only listened to what it said without the opportunity to respond to it. I waited for a moment for one of my classmates to raise his or her hand. It did not appear courteous for me to be the only one answering the questions. Fair enough, a girl raised her hand.

"Some citizens could run for offices, become members of the government, and help run the country," the girl said.

"This is wonderful! I think this class knows what to say when it comes to citizenship. What else could the citizens do to make the nation great?" the teacher continued.

I waited for a moment, but raised my hand when no one else did. I noticed that some students had something to say, but hesitated to raise their hands. It was not unusual for students to dither from speaking out. They hesitated to talk for different reasons. Some knew the answers, but did not know how to explain them. Some thought their classmates would laugh at them if they got the answers wrong. Others simply lacked the confidence to speak out when other students were listening.

"Go ahead, Ayodele, tell us another way to support our country," Mrs. Olafunmiloye instructed me.

"The citizens should pay their taxes promptly," I added to the discussion on citizenship.

"That's very good of you! I was expecting that. It is important for the people to pay their taxes, so the government could have money to provide electricity, water, good roads, schools, and the other things needed by the people," the teacher explained as simply as she could.

I wanted the discussion to continue because I had something to say about diverse topics. Apart from listening to the *rediffusion*, I had been reading the newspapers and soft-sell magazines brought home by Uncle Biodun and Uncle Sunday. I sometimes read the *Daily Times*, *Sketch*, *Tribune*, *Drum*, *Spear*, *West Africa*, *Gboungboun*, and *Atoka Yoruba* whenever the two uncles gave me their old papers. I also bought the educational periodical named *Aworerin* at school, whenever Grandma had the money.

"Now, I have a tricky question for the class," said Mrs. Olafunmiloye. "Do you really think that the students who have no jobs, don't pay taxes, and are not in positions of authority could give something back to the nation?"

The Hidden Treasures in Gray Hair

A student raised his hand almost immediately, and the teacher pointed at him. He attempted to answer the question based on how it sounded. He probably did not take into account the fact that the teacher described the question as tricky in the first place. He would not have answered the way he did if he had thought about the teacher's warning.

"Students have no jobs. They don't pay taxes. They are not in positions of authority. So, they cannot give anything back to the country. Young people depend on their parents and relatives... They have nothing to offer," the boy explained.

I understood why the boy answered the question the way he did. Ordinarily, jobless people had no money to give to others. However, I thought young people had a lot to give back to the country, regardless of being jobless and not paying taxes. I was not alone in reasoning that way. It was obvious that the teacher had a different opinion, too. It appeared like she creased her brow inadvertently as she listened to the boy's argument.

It was also clear that some of the students objected to the boy's explanation. Some mumbled their opposition to the student's answer. A couple of the students attempted to verbalize their objection by talking at the same time. That did not go down well with the teacher. She expected students to raise their hands, and be recognized before talking. Mrs. Olafunmiloye urged everyone in the classroom to respect the class 'rule of decorum. We all agreed to her request.

"All of the citizens have something to give, regardless of their ages or social status. Being young or not having a job shouldn't prevent a good citizen from giving something back to the country..."

Mrs. Olafunmiloye was still explaining that every citizen had something to offer when the unusual happened. A girl named Funmilayo fainted and fell to the floor. There was a pandemonium in the classroom, as the incident was so strange. No one knew what to do immediately. The teacher yelled for someone to call the headmaster (the elementary school principal). The class captain went for the headmaster, and a few others went to call other teachers.

Mrs. Olafunmiloye splashed some cold water on Funmilayo's face and started fanning her. The remaining students flocked together and watched in amazement. Nothing like that had happened in the classroom before that day. I simply prayed and hoped that the girl would wake up shortly. The look on everyone's face was deplorable. Some of us joined the teacher in fanning the girl with our notebooks. There was no "911" to dial. Surprisingly, Funmilayo stood up by herself moments later.

"What happened?" the surprised girl asked the shocked students and the stunned teacher who were fanning her.

"Don't bother about what happened; I'll tell you later. Just sit down and rest for a while," the

The Hidden Treasures in Gray Hair

teacher reassured Funmilayo. The head teacher entered the classroom and soothed the dazed students.

"I applaud all of you for being good citizens. Being our brother's and sister's keepers is an attribute of good citizens. That's what you demonstrated. I'm pleased to notice that," the headmaster said to the class. I marveled at how what he said matched the class discussion earlier.

The head teacher said everyone should be glad that Funmilayo was okay, after all. He speculated that the girl probably passed out because of the unusually warm dry season. Then, he announced that all of the students in the class should go home for the rest of the day. The headmaster and the teacher remained with Funmilayo as the rest of the class departed gleefully. Each of us felt fulfilled for being seen as a good citizen.

The youths have a lot to offer their country, regardless of their economic or social status. They can give back to their nation indirectly. One may reason that a lot of youth have no jobs, do not pay taxes, and are not in positions of authority, but they give back somehow. The nation is better off when all of the citizens give back directly and indirectly. The youths may not be giving back to the nation directly, but giving back indirectly is better than not giving at all.

The youths who go to school regularly, pay attention to their studies, and respect the teachers and fellow students are giving back to their country indirectly. Arguably, they are doing something for the country by not allowing the money spent on education to go to waste. The money spent on education is an investment in the future generations of the country. Making judicious use of resources is productive, instead of allowing them to go to waste.

Taking advantage of what society offers and making good use of what the community gives are good for the country. The nation is assured that she has responsible youths to rely on in the future. The demeanor of today's youth is the sign of the kind of citizens to expect tomorrow. The nation with assiduous, appreciative, and dependable youths has good people to rely on in the future. On the other hand, the nation with idle and uninspired youths with a dependence mentality will have an uncertain future.

It is well with the country when the youths are law-abiding. Youths are giving back to their country indirectly when they do not violate the law. The resources for prosecuting juvenile offenders would go into good use if the youths do not overwhelm the legal system. It is the same when youths do not vandalize private and public properties. Vandalism may cost a country billions of dollars in a year. The money so spent wastefully could be spent on productive ventures.

Law-abiding youths give back to their country in other ways. They leave money in their parents' or guardians' pockets by saving them from paying legal fees. The youths also save their families' time and energy. The parents or guardians are more productive when they are able to go to work or do useful things at home, instead of accompanying their wards to court. The youths who respect the law and the people in positions of authority would likely remain good citizens in the future.

Healthy youths who do not engage in destructive lifestyles are giving back to their country. A nation loses a lot when her youth engages in illegal substance consumption. The money spent on treating such youths could be used for making life abundantly comfortable for the people. Drugs destroy people physically, mentally, and financially. The youths who destroy themselves with drugs would not likely grow up and be useful to the country.

Well-cultured youths who live disciplined lives are giving something back to their country. They are different from the youths who destroy or deface road signs and cause harm to road users thereafter. There have been stories of good citizens who got into nasty road accidents because some youth removed or defaced the road signs meant for warning the road users. Neighborhoods have been labeled, abandoned, and isolated because the youths defaced the walls with graffiti.

The youths who refrain from gang activities are giving back to their country indirectly. Countries lose a large number of young people to "gang wars" every year. The unnecessary pressure put on the nation, states, cities, and the neighborhoods could be avoided. The amount of resources invested in placating gang-involved youths could be used for something more productive. For instance, the police officers who struggle to prevent gang activities in a city could be used for other purposes.

Consequently, the adults had good reasons for requesting youths to be good citizens. The youths who pay attention to the priceless words of trustworthy adults will benefit from them. The guest speaker who once visited my elementary school had useful advice for the students. He reached out to the adults and the youths in a way they could not resist.

"The stability of the creeper is the pleasure of the bird that perches on it. The bird is stable if the climbing plant remains stable. However, the bird becomes unstable if the plant is unstable," the guest speaker began. "The calmness of our country is the pleasure of the people. The citizens are happy when the nation is peaceful. A country's future is guaranteed when it has peaceful and responsible youths. But, the people become miserable when the nation has many troublesome youths to contend with."

"Everyone has to give something back to the country. The government cannot do it alone, the rich cannot do it alone, the poor cannot do it alone, and the adults cannot do it alone. Remember, the child's hand is not long enough to reach the shelf, and the adult's hand is too big to enter through the mouth of the gourd. The youths and the adults must work together to get things done. The sky is large enough for all birds to fly. The country is large enough for all to support." The guest continued to advocate good citizenship.

"The citizens of every nation harvest what they sow. Those who defecate in the middle of the road on their way out will see flies on their way back home. The youths of today are the leaders of tomorrow. You will have a satisfying nation in the future if you give back to the country now. Don't listen to anyone who says you have nothing to offer because you are young. You have everything that your country wants from you now," the guest speaker concluded.

Once upon a time, there was a good-looking and sociable prince. He was a well-raised noble from a well-cultured royal home. Everyone respected and described the prince as a perfect picture of a good citizen. No one thought such a responsible prince would bring himself to ridicule till it happened.

The prince usually went to a private pond to swim on daily basis. Everything went on fine for a while till something wacky ensued. The young royal was swimming one midmorning when a mad man approached the pond. The mad man watched as the prince swam. He marveled at the prince's royal robe, slacks, and sandals. The mad man wished he was the prince. Although he had a mental problem, the mad man knew that the royal apparels were good.

"I have always wished to be a royal," thought the mad man. "Why can't I just dress like one, if I can't be one?"

The disturbed man grabbed the royal clothing and sandals. He glanced at the prince, and discovered that the latter was engrossed in swimming. He put on the royal robe, slacks, and sandals. The prince was not paying attention. The mad man imagined himself as the real prince. He decided to walk away from the pond with the prince's property and show them off to the people at the market place. The prince looked back at that point and saw the mad man going away with his possessions.

"Hey! You are wearing my robe," the prince yelled.

The mad man glanced at the prince and smiled as he walked away from the latter.

"I'm talking to you! Give me back my robe, slacks, and sandals," the prince yelled even louder.

Unfortunately, the mad man started running as he saw the prince coming after him. Then, the prince noticed that the other fellow was the mad man that usually sat under the tree in front of the palace. He gave the disturbed fellow a chase.

The Hidden Treasures in Gray Hair

"Help, someone! The mad man has robbed me of my possessions," the prince bawled as he ran naked, pursuing the mad man.

The mad man headed for the marketplace, running as fast as he could. He was bent on showing off the royal garments to everyone at the market. The prince was carried away by the passion to retrieve his possessions. Little did he realize that he was making himself the pawn of the crazy man, who wanted his own moments of fame.

The naked prince continued to chase the well-dressed mad man. The two men's appearances had changed. It was the mad man who used to be naked, and the prince used to dress nicely. Now, the prince was naked and the mad man was well-dressed. The two men ran into the market place. The prince was determined to retrieve his belongings, and the mad man was determined to show off the stolen royal apparels.

"Get my robes off of the mad man, someone. Please, help!" the panting prince yelled as the two men ran round the stalls at the marketplace.

The people were stunned. They were not sure why the naked man was calling the well-dressed man the mad one. They recognized the royal robe, but not the mad man. The mad man looked like the prince because he dressed like one. The prince appeared like the crazy man because he was naked like one. The people made the most obvious assumption, and presumed that the mad man was chasing the prince.

Everyone scampered in an attempt to help the "prince" and earn the king's favor. Some brandished cudgels, and others brought out whips. They ran after the two men, yelling at the supposed mad man to stop chasing the assumed prince.

"I'm the real prince," shouted the prince. Sadly, nobody believed him. The people kept asking him to stop chasing the prince.

"They called you a thief, and you continued to play with someone else's goat," said an elderly woman at the marketplace. "The people think you are the real mad man, and you continue to run around naked."

"I insist that I'm the real prince," maintained the prince.

"Well, the thief who steals the royal trumpet has no hidden place to blow it. We shall soon find out who is the real prince," the woman responded.

The people flogged the prince when he failed to stop chasing who they assumed to be the prince. It took the intervention of a royal messenger, who recognized the true prince as he reeled on the ground. The visibly embarrassed prince got his royal apparels back shortly. Unfortunately, it was too late; the out-of-the-blue deed was done.

Thereafter, people advised the prince never to act like an uncivilized person again. They were surprised that one of the best citizens in that kingdom inadvertently allowed a derailed man to de-

The Hidden Treasures in Gray Hair

ride him at the market place. Everyone admonished the prince, whom they thought of as an initiated citizen, to stop acting like an uninitiated citizen.

The lesson in this story is that good people should not allow bad people to make them engage in bad behaviors. Else, the former would be perceived as bad, too. Responsible citizens should not behave like, or partake in the destructive behaviors embraced by reckless citizens. Otherwise, the responsible citizens will be perceived as bad citizens. Good kids who copy or associate with irresponsible kids will be seen as irresponsible kids, too. The good kids of today should not act like bad kids, because they (the good kids) are the leaders of tomorrow.

Chapter 15
LEADERSHIP—The Humbling Mission

Leadership is a conscientious endeavor. It is the point where humanity meets humility. It is not about being the boss, but being firm and modest simultaneously. It goes beyond ordering people around, but by living in people's hearts.

Ibadan was a city with a difference. It was not just the capital of the Western Region of Nigeria; it was a fascinating city. It mesmerized the young and the old alike. Those who visited the city returned home with compelling stories. One of such stories was about the tall building that "made fun" of people. Onlookers' caps reportedly dropped behind their heads as they looked up to see the top of the skyscraper.

"*Ile Awosifila!*" began Rotimi, the barber's son, who had visited Ibadan. He attempted to explain how tall the building was. "They called it *Ile Awosifila* because the house was so tall that people's caps dropped off behind them as they tried to see the top." He tilted his head backward to emphasize how people looked at the top of the building. With a dash of his right hand behind his head, he demonstrated how people's hats fell off behind them.

Cocoa House was the first skyscraper in the region and the nation. Most people were quick to understand why the building was so named. Cocoa was the main cash crop and the backbone of that region's economy. Thus, the amazing building was named after the crop that laid the "golden eggs" in that region. Whoever went to Ibadan without seeing the *Cocoa House* was said not to have been to the city.

"The building was so tall that it poked the sky. My father said he had been to the other parts of the country, but he didn't see another building as tall as the *Cocoa House*," Rotimi continued with his explanation. "I'll probably move to that city when I complete my secondary education."

Rotimi was not the only child with the ambition of moving to the city. Most local youths had the aspiration to relocate to the city and become successful there. We couldn't stop imagining being part of the hustle and bustle that made the city tick. The supposedly "endless" streets and long chains of vehicles on the roads fascinated us so much.

"I can't wait to see the city with its many cars, and the '*go slow*' everywhere," said Adeniran, my distant cousin, referring to traffic jams in the city. "I wonder if those who have no cars trek in the city where the streets are so long and people travel long distances within the same metropolis."

"Of course, some people would trek or take public transportation," I said, with a certain level of confidence. "I don't think everyone in the city is rich enough to own a car. You'll be amazed that many of the people there trek to their destinations." I knew that many of the people in our town could not even afford bicycles. The city could not be an exception.

In addition to Cocoa House, Ibadan was reputable for having some other "firsts" that set it apart from most African cities of that epoch. People talked a lot about the premier University of Ibadan; the "massive" Liberty Stadium; the seemingly endless *Dugbe* Market; the legendary municipal building christened Mapo Hall; the television station; and *Ile Akede*, the radio station located at *Orita Bashorun*.

People hardly talked about Ibadan's infrastructure without talking about the "great" leader who made them possible. Chief Obafemi Awolowo, the Premier of Western Region, was known as the legend that made Ibadan tick. He was the topic of many discussions, and the iconic picture that most *Yorubas* wanted on their calendars. Every child wanted to have a glimpse of him when his convoy passed by the town several decades ago.

"Awo, the single elephant that shakes the forest," began my grandfather. He enjoyed hailing and talking about Chief Awolowo, the legendary leader of the *Yorubas*. "No one glances at the elephant and looks away. Whoever sees the elephant sees something impressionable."

Chief Awolowo, fondly called Awo by his numerous admirers, dominated the political landscape of the Western Region. He was an idol to both young and old. His image loomed over the other leaders in the region. The former leader's followers raised their own children to embrace the man the way they did. The adults told Chief Awolowo's story with a lot of passion.

"What if another leader emerges and displaces Chief Awolowo?" I asked my grandfather the question I knew he would dismiss with a wave of a hand.

"Displace? Who is tough enough to stop Awo?" Grandpa answered my question with another question. "The creeper that attempts to stop the elephant from having a drink from the brook will enter the water with the elephant. No one can challenge Awo and make him flinch. The tough dog calms down when it sees the tiger's eyes."

"Okay, Grandpa, what if those who opposed Chief Awolowo team up and dislodge him as the leader of the *Yorubas*?" I sometimes challenged my grandfather to witty debates on current affairs. The beauty of it was that we were both winners, as

The Hidden Treasures in Gray Hair

Grandpa made sure that the two of us came out of such discussions smiling.

"Awo's detractors may team up all they want, but they cannot match him. Two thousand sticks combined cannot match a single cotton-tree. What else do you want to know?" Grandpa teased me; he did not want the debate to end at that point.

"The forest was full of trees," he continued, "but *Iroko* stood out as the king of woods. There was buffalo in the field, but the lion emerged as the king of the plain. Awo's detractors were there before the people chose the man as their leader." My grandfather justified his support for the leader of the Yorubas.

"Another *Yoruba* leader would emerge when Chief Awolowo dies," I suggested with a tinge of certainty.

"You are right. A new leader would emerge when Mother Earth inters Awo. However, that won't happen in his lifetime. No one uses the bush-goat's skin for a drum when the animal is still alive. It has to be after it passes on."

I was not ready to give up the debate. I understood that my grandfather was enjoying himself, too. I was hoping for the happy ending that usually trailed our encounters. I knew that Grandpa would adjudge the two of us the winners when he noticed that I no longer had interest in the debate. I thought that might come soon if he continued to tackle my questions about his idol. Addition-

Dele Ajaja

ally, I enjoyed talking about leadership, because I thought I might become a leader someday.

"Will you be disappointed if Chief Awolowo lets you down?" I asked finally, knowing that my grandfather was a diehard Chief Awolowo's supporter.

"Every mortal is fallible, but Awo has demonstrated leadership for decades. I don't expect him to let the people down at this level." Grandpa tried to explain that part philosophically. "As a member of the old guard, he knows that whoever borrows one thousand two hundred cowries without paying would have difficulty borrowing one thousand four hundred in the future. Awo won't trade the people's love and trust with a disappointment."

Grandpa brought the debate to a head at that point, with the usual verdict of two winners—the two of us. He commended my ability to engage in a healthy and respectful debate with adults. His compassion reminded me of the adage that the elderly would not allow the head of a baby to slump on his mother's back, at the market place. The mother who carried the baby on her back cannot see how his head rested, but the kind elder who noticed how awkward the baby's head rested would warn the mother.

My grandfather's praise for the leader he admired inspired me. I marveled at people's love and admiration for the leaders who stole their hearts. I thought about what made people show affection and devotion to some leaders, and dis-

The Hidden Treasures in Gray Hair

trust and odium for others. Something told me that the good leaders touched people's hearts, but the bad leaders broke people's hearts. I really wanted to be a leader; the one who touched people's hearts.

Leadership is not everyone's business, as it should be. It is meant for those who have the gift of service to the people. It is a serious undertaking for serious-minded people. Leadership is an endeavor for those who have human faces. It requires humility, compassion, tact, and a can-do spirit. Leadership is the trade of the man, woman, or child who can take the heat. It is the vocation of those who focus on the targets, and not what the *"armchair footballers"* say.

Armchair footballers are the spectators who sit and watch the real footballers. The *armchair footballers* do not play or sweat like the real players. They only sit, with bowls of snacks in their hands, and watch the players. Yet, they comment back and forth about the game. They act like they know how to catch, kick, or run with the ball more than the real players.

"That guy should have caught and run with the ball through the right flank," an *armchair footballer* would say.

Leadership is a privilege because everyone does not have the gift of leading. It is about rendering service to the people. It is not about being the boss or ordering people around. It is about taking charge and working for the common good of the people. Leaders are expected to touch people's lives positively, even when they have to give up personal pleasures.

Mankind has witnessed chains of leaders throughout history. Some leaders touched people's hearts by serving them. Some made life miserable by taking advantage of the people. Some caused wars and pains for the people. Others were neither good nor bad. History has made it possible for people to learn about the past leaders. The history books tell good stories about some leaders, and obnoxious stories about the others. The names of some leaders were consigned to a footnote of history because people did not know what to make out of them.

Mother Teresa, the 1979 Nobel Peace Prize winner, lived and died among the poor in Calcutta, India. She could have dined and wined with the queens and kings of her time. She could afford the luxury of living big on her own. Mother Teresa could have used her fame and status to acquire dealings and opulence. However, she chose to be modest, and became a mother to those who needed a caring mother.

Rosa Louise Parks, the mother of modern-day civil rights movement, rose to prominence by rejecting man's inhumane treatment against others. She did that at the expense of her personal comfort. History books say that Mrs. Parks, a black woman, refused to give up her seat to a white man

The Hidden Treasures in Gray Hair

on a bus, in the segregated city of Montgomery, Alabama. That single act of bravery led to the Bus Boycott of 1955, and the beginning of big protests against racism in the United States of America.

Lady Diana, the late Princess of Wales, mingled freely with AIDS patients around the world. She did not have to do that, but she did. She gave her heart to those rejected by the world. Thereafter, the appreciative admirers of Lady Diana christened her the "Princess of Hearts" for embracing the downtrodden everywhere. Prominence and possessions were not enough to stand between her and the desperate peoples around the world.

Mahatma Gandhi, the unpretentious nonviolent activist, was the founding father of modern India. He embraced a peaceful resolution to the colonization of his homeland by another land—England. Gandhi could have embraced violence to free his people, but he chose peaceful diplomacy. His peaceful engagements influenced others around the world thereafter.

Dr. Martin Luther King Junior, the 1964 Nobel Peace Prize winner and icon of American civil rights activism, embraced peace, too. He had good reasons to be outraged, but chose nonviolence for resolving the problem of segregation in the U.S. Thus, he earned himself the love and appreciation of fellow countrymen, women, and children. Now, the Americans and the world celebrate Dr. King on the third Monday of January every year.

Dele Ajaja

Nelson Mandela, the legendary conscience of Africa, who shared the 1993 Nobel Peace Prize with former Prime Minister Frederik de Klerk, helped to end apartheid peacefully in South Africa. He decided to love those who hated him. Mandela thought there was an alternative to hatred. He understood that an eye for an eye would make everyone blind in the end. He forgave and called for a better future for all South Africans.

Cesar Estrada Chavez was a civil rights and labor leader. He led the struggle to procure better treatment for migrant workers in the U.S. That marked the beginning of better life for migrant workers in the country.

Henry Bill Gates of the U.S. is one of the heroes of our time. He is one of the most conscientious wealthy people in history. He chose to make life bearable for the poor. Meanwhile, a number of rich people flaunt their inordinate wealth in a cold world full of poverty.

Morris Seligman Dees of the Southern Poverty Law Center, Montgomery, Alabama, understands the essence of liberty. He is the acclaimed leader who fights hatred and promotes civil rights in the U.S. and the world. He did not restrict himself to his race. He refused to limit his horizons, and chose the world as his constituency.

Permit me to use the story I invented to illustrate the beauty of leadership and service to the people.

The Hidden Treasures in Gray Hair

Once upon a time, all of the warriors in the world commenced a journey to the land of spirits. It was mandatory for them to give stewardship of their roles in the world. The spirits were superior to humans. The warriors left in opulence and splendor. Their servants carried them in expensive and colorful palanquins. Trumpets were blaring, and the overzealous servants whipped ordinary people away from the road.

"Make way for special people!" the servants screamed as loud as they could.

The sun shined with all of its brilliance and the clouds fizzled out to make way for the mighty and powerful warriors of the world. Back in the land of the spirits, the king was surrounded by his chiefs as he awaited the mortal warriors. Compared to earthly palaces, the palace of the king of spirits was more beautiful in all ways. The king's trumpet blowers were second to none.

The worldly warriors' henchmen had no chance, compared to the powerful henchmen of the king of spirits. The earthly warriors' servants became fearful as they approached the gate of the city of the spirits. Everything over there surpassed that of the world manyfold. The warriors' entourages appeared like packs of rats going to the lion's den. All of the worldly beings were awed in trepidation.

The warriors and their *yes-men* (the kowtowing servants) did soul-searching as they approached the gate of the spirits. The majority of

them knew they had done despicable things that the king of spirits would not appreciate. Then, they started singing:
All that I did wrong
Let me make them right
Before entering his presence
Offenders cannot stand by him
The king of spirits is just
All that I did wrong
Let me make them right

The warriors and their servants stopped at the gate shortly. They became powerless instantly as the gatekeeper waved his magic wand at them. The worldly judges were about to enter the city of the judge of the spirits.

"Silence! Silence! Silence!" the gatekeeper ordered the worldly party.

The warriors shook with fear in front of the gatekeeper. They imagined what would happen when they arrived in front of the king of the spirits himself. The gatekeeper opened the gate for the warriors and denied entry to their servants. He insisted that the warriors must stand before the king of spirits by themselves, without the worldly praise-singers.

The warriors' entourages had no option other than to heed the gatekeeper's command. They returned to the earth where they belonged, leaving the once-powerful warriors to their fates. The warriors were about to experience what they made their subjects go through on earth. Sud-

The Hidden Treasures in Gray Hair

denly, they realized that nothing was permanent, except change that kept coming.

One of the misfortunes of man was his potential to forget the past so soon. Man learned very little from history. He kept going after the same things that led to the downfall of those before him. The warriors' servants forgot what they witnessed at the gate of the spirits as soon as they returned to their different kingdoms. They selected new warriors, and they continued with the corrupt ways of the old.

Back in the land of the spirits, the warriors came before the king one after the other. It was time to render accounts of all they did while on earth. The warrior of the land where some of the citizens terrified the world was the first to go before the king. He expected the king of spirits to be pleased with him, because he did not find anything wrong with his style of administration. Nevertheless, he felt miserable as he was powerless.

"Why did you terrify my creations?" the king of the spirits enquired from the warrior whose subjects terrorized the people on earth.

"Your Honor, I was only the leader," began the worldly warrior. "I did not terrify anyone. I acknowledge that some of my subjects committed the crime for which I'm being charged."

The warrior could not figure out why he should pay for the crime committed by his citizens. He forgot that someone had to take responsibility for the evils done under his watch. The leader usually took the praise or the blame for his team's actions. The warrior tried harder to absolve himself from the acts of malevolence committed by some of his citizens.

"Whoever said you were not liable for the crimes committed by your followers was wrong," interrupted the king. "You had the authority, but did little to stop your followers from terrifying my creatures."

"I tried all I could to be upright. I did not terrify fellow humans. Please, pardon me." The warrior tried to dissuade the king of spirits from punishing him, but to no avail.

"A warrior is not answerable only to what he did. He also pays for the good deed he left undone," the king of the spirits explained. "You have no idea how your youths blew up themselves and innocent people, believing they would go to heaven for so doing." The king of the spirits ordered the warrior to endless terms of chastisement, because he did not do enough to stop his followers from engaging in violence.

Thereafter, the king of the spirits ordered his servants to escort another warrior to his presence. They brought the most powerful warrior who had the authority to make the world a better place, but failed to do so. He had the clout to instill social justice in the world, but lacked the will to do it. Again, this warrior felt like he did nothing wrong while on earth.

The Hidden Treasures in Gray Hair

"Do you recall the endless rhetoric you made about making the world a better place?" The king took the warrior back to the long promises he made about banishing injustice from the surface of the earth. "What about when you harbored the wealth stolen from poor nations, which resulted in innocent children dying of hunger? Your kingdom supplied deadly weapons to lands that needed food. Do you remember the toxic waste your nation dumped at helpless nations?"

The king adjudged the second warrior as a mean fellow. He sentenced him like the first warrior. Then, the king sent for the warrior who stole from his own people. Everyone knew how that warrior stole from his own land and transferred the wealth to other kingdoms. Just like the others before him, this warrior tried to justify his actions before the king of the spirits.

"Can you provide me an explanation for your wicked and disgraceful actions?" asked the king. The greedy warrior's eyes opened piously, and he realized that he did not need all of the stolen wealth after all. Both rich and poor people were the same in the land of spirits. The warrior deeply regretted his rapacious tendencies, but it was too late for him to mend his impious ways.

"Didn't you hear that vanity upon vanity is all vanity?" the king asked the warrior. The former reminded the latter about the adversity he exposed his own people to. The now powerless warrior looked foolish in front of a more powerful authority, which could make him pay for his wrongdoings. He attempted to beg for forgiveness, but the king was not persuadable.

"I'll right every wrong I committed if you give me one more chance, Your Honor," begged the warrior.

"There are no more chances once people cross over to the land of spirits. You cannot escape from the consequences designed for your immoral actions. See the traumatized faces of the innocent children who died of starvation because you robbed your land blind. Look at the faces of the youth who lost everything because you squandered their future." The king of spirits ordered the warrior to an everlasting term of repulsion.

The humble and selfless warrior who lived a life of service to his people came last. Many of his people appreciated his service, but those he disallowed from robbing the land did not. His detractors insulted and did everything they could to tarnish his sincere efforts. They even used his humble antecedent against him. The warrior placed his people first. He guarded his land's reputation like his own baby. He understood the idea of working for the common good of the people.

"Welcome to the infinite pleasure reserved for leaders with mission and vision," affirmed the king of spirits. "It takes thoughtful leaders to surrender worldly vanities for the ceaseless satisfaction that comes with the life of service to the people." The king offered a generous handshake to the responsible warrior. Once again, the king waved his magical wand, and the warrior was able to see the contented faces of his citizens on earth.

Back on earth, the good warrior's subjects were mournful, but decided to celebrate the life and times of their departed benevolent warrior. People praised the warrior in the streets. There was joy in the land of spirits as well. All of the spirits took turn to shake hands with the thoughtful warrior. There was a huge celebration in honor of the honest warrior. He knew that his people would appreciate his kindness and honesty, but he did not realize that the spirits would be grateful to him, too. The good leader lived happily ever thereafter.

I encourage all youths to aspire to be leaders—benevolent leaders with human faces. Young people should aspire to become the good leaders who will make the world a better place for all. After all, today's children are the leaders and the hope of tomorrow. God bless the good leaders everywhere.

Now that you have read this book, please, pay attention to the counsels of the dependable adults in your life. Those golden words could be useful to you at some points in life. Additionally, tell your friends about the wisdom you learned from the book. Children and young adults would understand life better if they learn from the responsible adults around them. Thereafter, they would not stumble on the tricky roads of life.

Dele Ajaja

I wish you the very best, my friend.
Thank you so much for your time.
© Dele Ajaja 2010.

Index

A
Abiose, 178–181
academic standing versus character, 43–44
accountability, 189, 192–194, 196, 197–207
achievement, friends' role in, 76
actions, consequences of, 56–57
Ade, 63–70
Adekunle, Benjamin, 235
Adeniran, 238
adults
    respect for, 140–141, 149
    and youths working together, 261
affluent people. See rich people
African Americans, 104
African self-determination, 104–105
airplane, invention of, 219
Aja (dog in Yoruba), 145, 146–149
alcohol, 65, 176, 179, 210
anger, 32, 97, 100–103, 105–113, 169
apartheid, 105, 276
armchair footballers, 273
armed robbery, 69
atomic elements, 143–144
authority, challenging, 13, 14

B
Baba James, 233
Baba Olaoba, 42
Baba Sao, 234
bank manager, 7
beauty, character and, 39, 42, 56
bees in folktales, 222, 225
Bell, Graham, 219–220
Biafra, 231–232, 235
big cities, 22
Biodun, 254
birds in folktales, 181–187, 222, 226–227
black pedestrian, accidental hitting of, 164–167
Bliss, 239–240
breakfast, 3
bricklaying, 238
bullying, 99, 101, 102, 212, 214
Bus Boycott of 1955, 274–275

C
cattle egrets, 20–21
challenges, overcoming, 17–18
character, 38, 39, 42, 43–57, 142, 236
Chavez, Cesar Estrada, 276
Chief Ayeleso, 43, 44
Chief Obafemi Awolowo, 269–272
children
    activities of, 59–63
    with disabilities, 98–103
    marriage and, 82–83
    nature of, 21–22, 151–154

chores, 19–20
cigarettes, 65–57
citizenship, 252–265
clocks, 77–80
Cocoa House (skyscraper), 268, 269
conduct, 198
conscience, 235
courage, 231, 233–248
crocodiles in folktales, 223, 229
cultures, 156

D
dating, 12, 13, 14, 17
Dayo, 97–103
Debisi, 174–178, 181, 240
Dees, Morris Seligman, 276
discipline
    courage and, 236
    defined, 181
    lack, consequences of, 171, 173–174, 175–180, 185–187
    students and, 39–42, 67–68, 81–82
disease, lack of wisdom compared to, 19
distractions, 12, 13
district officer, education of, 4
diversity, 155, 157
Divine's Will (folktale character), 242–248
dogs in folktales, 145, 146–149
dreams for future, 171, 172–173, 192
drugs, 13, 16, 18, 122, 174, 177–178, 210, 259

E
Edison, Thomas, 219
education
    before versus after raising family, 82–86
    hunger, overcoming through, 3–4, 16–17
    importance of, 1, 17–18, 194–197
    perseverance and, 217–218
    self-expression and, 15
    success linked to, 5–7, 10, 194
Eiffel Tower, 117
elders
    as education advocates, 197
    respect for, 140–141
electricity, discovery of, 219
elephants in folktales, 123–133
equality, 192
ethnic groups, 154, 157, 231–232
ethnic jokes, 157
experience, 22–23
expressing one's self, 14–15, 18

F
Falah, 121
families, respect for, 139–140
family of Dele Ajaja, education of, 83, 85, 115–116, 196
famine in folktales, 47–57, 73–75, 144–147, 181–187
farming, education and, 195–196
fathers, songs about, 135, 139
fingernails, white spots on, 20–21
folktales

    on anger, 105–113
    on character, 46–57
    on citizenship, 261–265
    on courage, 242–248
    on discipline, 181–187
    on friendship, 199–207
    on not wasting time, 86–96
    on perseverance, 220–230
    on pride, 123–133
    on respect, 144–149
    on wisdom, 29–38
Folu, 2
football, 62
friends, choice of, 59, 62–75, 97–100, 241–242
friendship in folktales, 199–207
Funmilayo, 256–257
Fun'yo, 171, 172–174, 181

G
Gandhi, Mahatma, 103, 275
gangs, 13, 16, 18, 259–260
Gates, Henry Bill, 276
Gbade, 70–75
generosity, 65
getting lost, 151–153
goals, focusing on, 12
golden rule, 56
good side in everyone, 209, 213–215
good triumph over evil, 28
Gowon, Yakubu, 235
grandfather clocks, 78–79

Grandma
- on accountability, 192–193, 197
- on choosing friends, 63–64, 65, 68
- on courage, 239
- on importance of education, 1, 3–4, 10, 16–17, 196
- on money, 23–25
- on open-mindedness, 157–162, 163–164, 167, 168, 169
- relatives of, 115–116
- respect for, 137
- stealing discouraged by, 46
- travels with, 189–190

Grandpa
- on accountability, 193–194
- as Chief Obafemi Awolowo supporter, 270–272
- courage of, 232–234
- on creating own path, 239
- education, attitude concerning, 4, 194–195, 196, 197
- as farmer, 8, 27, 195
- respect for, 137–139
- time, attitude toward, 80
- wisdom of, 25–29, 38

grandparents, listening to, 23, 158, 192, 197–198
Great Wall of China, 117
greed, consequences of, 47–57

H
harmattan (cold and hazy season), 2, 19

higher education, 196
HIV, 174
home, sayings about, 249
humans versus elephant, 125–126, 127, 129–133
humility, 28, 236
hunger
    famine, 47–57, 73–75, 144–147, 181–187
    folktales about, 47–57, 91–96
    overcoming, 3–4, 16–17
hyenas in folktales, 222–223, 227

I
Ibadan (capital city), 251, 267–269
Igbos, 163–164, 231
Ijapa Tiroko (tortoise in folktales), 47–57, 86–96, 106–113, 126–133, 185–187
Ilesha (city), 190
illusory things, 191–192
inventors, 219–220
Itu (feat), 209–215
Iwaraja (town), 190

J
jobs, education role in obtaining, 4

K
kerosene, 238–239
King, Martin Luther, Jr., 104, 275
Klerk, Frederik de, 276

L
Lady Diana, 275
Lagos (city), 78, 79
law-abiding youth, 258–260
laziness, consequences of, 70–73, 74–75, 86–96
LB, 122
leadership, 267, 269–283
lekeleke (cattle egrets), 20–21
lifestyles, rejecting destructive, 239, 240, 259
light bulb, invention of, 219
lion in folktales, 30–38
London Bridge, 116
lunch, no money for, 3

M
mad men in folktales, 261–265
magazines, 254
Mama Oye, 78
Mama Talabi, 153
Mandela, Nelson, 104–105, 276
manners, 198
manual labor, 238
marijuana, 177–178, 210
marriage
    and children, 82–83
    laziness effect on, 88–96
meals, 3
mistrust, 155
model cars and trucks, 61
money
    earning, 237–239

lending, folktales about, 106–112
saving and spending, 23–25
mothers
    eating (in folktales), 145–149
    songs about, 135–136, 139
Mother Teresa, 274
Mr. Fakayode, 116
Mr. Fasakin, 81, 82–84
Mr. Ogundana, 44
Mr. Olorunfemi, 142–143, 144
Mrs. Olafunmiloye, 252–256
Ms. Ogunrinde, 103, 105

N
national youth service, 162, 163
newspapers, 254
newspaper vendor, troublesome, 210–213
New York, trip to, 21–22
Nigerian civil war, 231–235
Nigerian national anthem, 251
Nkrumah, Kwame, 104
nonviolence, 103–105, 275

O
Oga Ayo "Ko-Large," 232
Oga Femi, 238
Oga Imisi, 4, 238
okoto (spinning top), 60–61
Olatimilehin, S.O. (Samuel Olaiya), 216–220
Olorun (creator of heaven and earth), 30
Olubadan (ruler of Ibadan), 250–251

Omoluwabi (a dependable person), 198
opponent, turning into supporter, 162, 163, 167, 168–169
orphans in folktales, 220–230
Oyinbo (a light-skinned person), 6, 12

P
Panama Canal, 118
parents
    education of, 83, 85
    respect for, 135–136, 144–145
Parks, Rosa Louise, 274–275
Parthenon, 117
patriotism, 252. See also citizenship
peace, promoting, 192
peer pressure, 12, 13
perseverance, 214–215, 216–230
pigs in folktales, 106–113
plant life cycle, human success and, 8
poor home, growing up in, 59
popular boys and girls, 176
pride
    excessive, 28, 175–176
    before fall, 37–38, 118
    in family members, 115
    pretty side of, 116–118
    ugly side of, 118–133
princes in folktales, 261–265
punctuality, 39, 80–81
pyramids of Giza, 116

R
race, 154, 156, 158–159, 160, 164–167
racism, fight against, 275
rainy season, 2–3
recreational drugs, 16
rediffusion, 249–252, 253, 254
religions, 154, 156, 159–160
respect, 135, 139–149
rich children, 5–6
rich people, 4–6, 77, 78, 79
riddles, solving, 61–62
right and wrong, sense of, 235
role models, inappropriate, 13
romance, 12, 17
Rotimi, 267–268

S
saving for rainy day, 23–24
school, staying in, 216–220
School Board Disciplinary Committee, 42
school dropouts, 6, 68–70
school transfer, 43
self-esteem, 15
self-respect, 141–142
Shah Jaha, 117
shoes, lack of, 1, 3, 6, 17
slavery, history of, 165
smoking, 65–57, 176, 179
snobbish soap opera star, 121–122
soccer, 62
social justice, 192, 280

Soji, 115–116
South Africa, 104–105
Sphinx, 116
spinning tops, 60–61
sporting activities, 62
Statue of Liberty, 116–117
status, consequences of increased, 119–120
stealing, 45–46, 63–64, 68–69
students
    as citizens, 254–257, 258
    discipline, 39–42, 67–68, 81–82
    as leaders, 41
success
    courage and, 236
    discipline required for, 171, 173
    education role in, 5–7, 10, 194
    path to, 13
    perseverance and, 215–216
    plant life cycle and human, 8
    pride interference with, 120
    requirements for, 102
summer break, 171–172
Sunday, 254
survival, 7–8
Swan, Joseph, 219
Sydney Harbor Bridge, 118

T
tailor apprentice, Grandma advice to, 24–25
Taj Mahal, 117
talented youth, pride as pitfall of, 120–123, 174–

178
tall building, 267–268
taxes, paying, 254
teachers
    power struggles with, 13, 67–68, 122, 175
    respect for, 39–41, 142–144, 257–258
telephone, invention of, 219–220
time, lessons about, 14, 77, 80, 82–96
toddlers, 151–153
tolerance, 151, 153–154, 156–169
tortoises in folktales, 29, 30–38, 47–57, 86–96, 106–113, 123–133, 146, 147–149, 181–187
toys, homemade, 59–61
travels, 189–191
trustworthiness, 45–46
truth, 28, 168, 231
turning life around, 180–181
Tutu, Desmond, 105

U
uncles, 2, 4, 65, 115–116, 254
underprivileged children, 5, 237
United Nations Organization (UNO), 154
United States, arrival in, 168–169
University of Ibadan, 269

V
values, 16
vandalism, 258, 259
video games, 16
violence

alternatives to, 103–105
among youth, 13
leadership and, 280
negative consequences of, 102, 105–106, 169

W
wasting time, 14
wisdom, 19, 23, 25–29, 32, 36, 38
wooden clocks, 77–78
world, making a better place, 161–169, 280–281
wrestling, 62
Wright brothers, 219

Y
yam, parable of, 7–12, 13, 15
Yorubas
    families, 139, 141
    as farmers, 232
    hospitality, 240
    leaders, 269, 270, 271
    sayings of, 164
young man, Grandpa's advice to, 26–27
youth
    as citizens, 257–261
    as leaders, 273, 283
    violence among, 13, 280

Made in the USA
Columbia, SC
19 April 2019